# SHAMAN'S WISDOM

......................................................

## Reclaim Your Lost Connection
with the Universe

# SHAMAN'S WISDOM

·············································

## Reclaim Your Lost Connection
## with the Universe

·····················

**Tony Samara**

FINDHORN PRESS

First published by Findhorn Press 2009

ISBN: 978-1-84409-159-1

British Library Cataloguing-in-Publication Data.
A catalogue record for this book is available from the British Library.


Edited by Jane Engel
Cover design by Damian Keenan
Layout by Prepress-Solutions.com
Printed and bound in the European Union


1 2 3 4 5 6 7 8 9 10 11 12 13 14 13 12 11 10 09

Published by
Findhorn Press
305A The Park,
Findhorn, Forres
Scotland IV36 3TE

Tel +44(0)1309 690582
Fax +44(0)131 777 2711
eMail info@findhornpress.com
www.findhornpress.com

# Table of Contents

# Acknowledgements

My deepest gratitude goes to Christian Ghasarian for his time and vital work in transforming my manuscript into this book. I would also like to thank Muriel of Sydney, Maery and Venetia of "Morningswood" and all of the other kind people who helped to put the jigsaw puzzle pieces together; helping to bring this ancient knowledge into the modern world for you all to enjoy. Of course, none of this would have been possible without the patience and understanding of my wife, Sylvia, and my children, Sai, Shara and Tavi.

# Preface

As we live in such changing and strange times, the key to one's self can become lost in the many opposing messages, passions and feelings we confront daily, often with resulting stress, sickness and unhappiness.

I realised that this conflict, which I had also experienced, was Western culture not respecting the inner process that I call healing. This book is about that process.

I hope that this book unlocks your heart and opens you to a world that ancient and shamanic cultures valued. I also hope this book encourages you with effective tools and joyful wisdom.

I thank you for reclaiming your lost connection with the Universe.

# Introduction

During my childhood, I suffered from a blood disease similar to anaemia. I was weak and so was my immune system. This is perhaps what allowed me to see the inside of things, in an unusual manner for a child of my age living in the Western world. In indigenous cultures such sicknesses would often be seen as the start of a profound process, which could lead to initiation.

One day, a powerful dream revealed to me that it is not the external world that supports us but a very deep force coming from inside. In this dream, I saw a chair made of gold at the top of a beautiful hill. Somebody, with whom I was working, asked me whether it was mine. I answered negatively and he said to me: "Why don't you sit on the chair?" So, I did. Then I burst into tears. All my being, in that moment understood that life is nourishing us all the time and that the world belongs to us. Through this dream my view of the world was changed irrevocably forever, preparing me for the future events, of which at that time I was consciously unaware.

As a teenager, I had a conflict within as I endeavoured to become "normal" and to adjust myself to what seemed to me suitable in the Western world I lived in. Yet, I was feeling that a part of me could not nor did not want to be forced to take a path that was not mine. Doctors and psychologists were of practically no help to me. I started to develop an interest in philosophy and religion and discovered Buddhism in which I found a way to nourish my heart. I learned how to meditate at fifteen years of age and later entered a Zen Buddhist monastery located on the top of a beautiful Californian mountain, close to San Bernardino, where the air was pure and the food healthy. I became vegetarian and didn't become sick anymore. These experiences allowed me to realize that my former conflicts simply arose from the ignorance of the Western culture to the inner process of healing and spiritual development.

However, after two years, Buddhism appeared too easy for me. Even though the regimen was extremely severe (with meditation starting at 3:00am and the day often not ending until close to midnight), and for the first 6 months sitting in Full Lotus Position was, for me, complete agony. I felt well in the monastery but my inner voice was telling me to practice the harmony I found inside, in the outside world. Thus it was that I left the monastery for New York City and then London. The shock was enormous. Buddhism had not given me a complete vision of things. The external world was – and still is – very sick. It is easy to see the beauty of things when one lives in a beautiful environment but it is completely different when one is amidst the harshness and chaos of cities like New York. My inner peace had been connected to and supported by the harmonious everyday life of the monastery. I felt unfulfilled in these 'concrete jungles' and having always had a deep love for the sea and its creatures, I went to Australia to study Marine Biology.

After one year at University, I wished to put the theory into practice. I felt drawn "to save" the Amazonian rainforest and to help in one way or another to prevent its destruction. I wrote to a conservation organization based in Brazil. Six months later, I received a letter from the upper Amazon, close to Peru and Bolivia, inviting me to work with a small organization in a part of the forest, which was being quickly destroyed. I left Australia with the intent to work for the safeguard of the Amazonian rainforest.

A little while later, I found myself in a village inhabited by famous Ayahuascero shamans (shamans working with the healing Amazonian plant called Ayahuasca) which made me go through deep experiences of transformation. Slowly, I realized that these shamans had called me there and that the various experiences I shared with them had as their purpose the need to take their knowledge outside and to share it with the rest of the world, particularly the Western world.

# From the Rainforest to the Andes

· · · · · · · · · · · · · · · · · · ☆ ☆ ☆ · · · · · · · · · · · · · · · · · · ·

My first intense experience of the Amazon, in this dimension and in another totally extraordinary dimension of consciousness, took place a few days after my arrival. I was in a canoe, which was going down a river. There were many people staring at me and I had many thoughts going through my head. Time appeared to have come to a standstill. It rained a lot. The sounds of nature were everywhere. I was full of fears and doubts.

I thought I was very well prepared for the rainforest. I had spent six months improving my physical fitness at a gymnasium. I had immersed myself in the Spanish language with the help of books and language tapes. I had bought a machete, a hammock and a compass but oh, how the mosquitoes constantly bit me. Our canoe had been a tree a little time before and, in order to avoid sinking, we had to bail out the water continuously. Every time we hit a rock or a log I felt it was going to tip over. I began to wonder if this was the sanest thing to be doing at this time of my early twenties.

My westernized mind was full of fearful thoughts: "What if I have to go to hospital? How would I get there? Why are these people so satisfied with their life? Is this the paradise that I envisioned?"

While I was seeking thousands of excuses to leave the Amazon and to return to "civilization," a man at the front of the canoe pushed a tree branch away and was stung by a swarm of vicious bees. My initial reaction was to think "How lucky that it was not me," a feeling accompanied with pity and concern for the man who was suffering. The other people on the canoe laughed and behaved in a way that was incomprehensible to me. I was in a culture very different from all that I had known before.

I asked my fellow travellers: "Why laugh at suffering?" (If they were not all shamans, they lived in a shamanic culture.) They answered my question with another question: "Can true compassion be understood through feelings of fear, negativity and doubt?"

It was explained to me that the energy body of the man mortally stung by the bees was already in fear and pain and that my own fears and doubts brought only more negativity to his energetic body; that true compassion consists in helping the person to free himself from pain.

"By laughing, we helped to pull the fear out from the body of this man who was already in a state of shock and in danger of dying. If all of the passengers in the canoe had reacted as you did, their egocentric thoughts would have fed this negativity and the man would certainly have died," said one of my companions.

I realized that each one in the canoe except me had been present to the situation from a healing point of view rather than from the ego. Their laughter was an expression of this healing energy. My cultural programming had been different and from that moment, I seriously began to question my beliefs about this culture that the Western world would describe as "primitive."

Slowly, I understood that I had come to the Amazon not "to save the rainforest" – the idea which had motivated me at the beginning – but to save a part of myself I had almost forgotten about: my deepest Being. The ego is very skilful in creating tempting diversions from our true mission on earth. In the "civilized" world, it can be animated by many very creditable goals like " saving the rainforest." In spite of my great love for nature, a nature that I had studied in detail from my childhood to my University classes, I did not feel really at ease in the forest.

To save the rainforest implied to understand it and, in the end, to understand myself.

Our relationship to natural law is the most important aspect of shamanic cultures. For this reason Ayahuasceros see *Pachamama* (Mother Earth) as a living spiritual guide, who provides balance in all aspects of life. In Western societies, on the other hand, the earth is rarely considered this way because one is conditioned by fear, which in itself is an illusion. We constantly seek outside of ourselves for the means to find harmony inside of our mind, our body and our emotions, little realizing that harmony constitutes the paramount force of each living thing. This sense of connectedness with everything is the primordial state of humankind.

∞

I had spent several years practicing deep meditation but I had never known the type of magical relationship with nature maintained by some people in societies labelled as "primitive." For Ayahuasceros in particular, the rainforest is an intrinsic part of themselves. This perception of reality gives a childlike innocence to most of the shamanic communities I lived with.

Anthropologists have for a long time called into question the concept of "primitiveness" by realising that it may not be so. What can be said about a "civilization" which is unaware of the natural laws? By being satisfied with their existence and freedom, by not needing to harm themselves or compete against others and the world that surrounds them in their search for happiness, indigenous communities express an example completely missing in centers of Western "civilization" such as New York City and London.

∞

Days went by. The shamans invited me to take Ayahuasca mixed with different plants, along with other specific foods (i.e. bananas, manioc, etc). My body was transforming itself. I thought I had been purifying it by consuming healthy food and by detoxifying it through fasting. But one day, to my great surprise, I was told that my body was polluted, that it carried the weight of its past, and that the Ayahuasceros could feel it. They started preparing nauseous decoctions of plants that made me vomit for seven days. My entire body became weak.

I was aware however that my vomiting did not operate simply on the physical level: on another level, I was also extracting the negativity of my mind. Through the vomiting, I eliminated diseases from the past. Under the guidance of the shamans, I could look at suffering in a new way and understand that it is caused by imbalance and that this imbalance should not be hidden because it is the key to healing. Healing is a transformation of mind and spirit that leads us to understand how to practice balance in our daily thoughts and deep emotions. The body is regarded here as the temple which contains the spirit.

I reached a stage where I let go of my mental and emotional programming. If, at the beginning, I had many doubts about the actions of the indigenous people in the forest, I gradually started to become like them. I was entering into the rhythm of the forest.

The shamans explained to me that all of the information we need is encoded in the depths our Being. Books are useless. It is enough to open oneself to this inner knowledge.

The process of weakening was a process of cleaning the body and also of connecting with the Spirit of the Forest. It was necessary for me to let go of the feeling of separation I had with the essence of life. The mystery of existence is that when one is ready for something, it happens! Ayahuasceros said to me that I was born to become a shaman and that they, with my consent, were going to initiate me.

My process of healing began with the purification of my body and culminated with my initiation.

Initiation is a fundamental dimension of shamanism. It does not depend on the quantity of time passed to learn but on releasing all of the points of reference that keep us separated from our essence. It does not lead to a diploma, as at the University, but brings up a process. For me, this process had started in my early childhood with my illness. I subsequently discovered that people who are selected to be shamans in shamanic societies are usually in some way ill or handicapped, like the "wounded healer" of many myths and legends. During my childhood, healing as being linked to spiritual reality had not been considered because this integral approach to physical and mental health had disappeared from "civilized" societies. Instead, a "band aid remedy" to my suffering had been sought through doctors, psychologists, etc.

∞

The shaman can start to work as a healer only when he goes through what is called an experience of death/rebirth, the death of suffering and the rebirth to a new way of seeing things, where the point of reference is not any more the ego but the Cosmos; everything being connected to everything. At the time of my initiation, I was given Ayahuasca and a terrible storm seized the forest and me. I had the greatest fear of my life. All my body disintegrated. I had the feeling I was going to die. I called upon the gods from various religions, in vain. A large snake appeared and started to swallow me. I understood that it represented the pulsation of the energy of the Universe. I lost the sense of my surrounding world and I was no longer afraid to die. My body had become a part of the Universe. I developed a feeling of unity.

This initiation changed all my perceptions of reality. Released of my past programming, my spirit was able to live the magic and the joy of existence.

When a balance is established between our personality and our soul-spirit, or higher self, a peace and an inner force allow us to experience the essence of things animate around us. The experience also brought me closer to my Amazonian companions and, from then on, I learned a lot about their beliefs of the world.

However, as the months passed by, little by little, I was detaching myself from this Amazonian knowledge with its dualistic conception of the world (good/bad, etc). The climate was also very difficult (being extremely humid) so I decided to leave and go to La Paz, in Bolivia. This meant leaving Amazonia and travelling to the Andes Mountains, close to Lake Titicaca.

Once there I started to work in the Quechua and Huachuma shamanic traditions, with people from various origins (Indian, African, Spanish, and Métis). The healing plant most used in the Andes was not Ayahuasca but San Pedro, a cactus that worked more gently. My Amazonian experiences had given me knowledge of many herbal remedies and now I was invited to expand my knowledge.

The lessons of Huachuma shamanism, which you will find in the remainder of this book, are based on old philosophies that can be traced back to Egypt.

Archaeologists have also found objects that prove that the Andean traditional ways of healing go back more than 5000 years.

I remember growing up in Egypt – a land steeped in history and forgotten cultures. I was immersed in traditional Egyptian society and went to the local school full of children and teachers who had grown up absorbing this unique blend of ancient customs and modern lifestyles.

I remember moments when visiting the pyramids on school expeditions. We were there of course to learn and understand all about the way of life during the days of the Ancient Egyptian Civilization but my memories are of the ancient artifacts.

There were lavishly adorned statues, linen-wrapped mummies in spectacular sarcophagi, hieroglyphic writings and wondrous jewels and ornaments depicting images of Gods, birds, plants, animals and scenes of daily life. As we were from the local school we were shown a glimpse of the treasures normally only accessible to archaeologists.

These deep memories came flooding back when I was in Trujillo, in Northern Peru, as I noticed remarkable resemblances between what I was seeing there and what I was remembering from Egypt.

Amazingly similar was the mythology, the pyramid-like structures, the hieroglyphs and the animal representations (such as cats). The innate feeling of the place was indistinguishable from that of my childhood memories.

All this spoke of a deeper connection between the two countries - a connection that was felt by me not only in the images but also in the spiritual aspects. Even in the ways of healing used in Peru today I could feel that the roots originated in Egypt. As I began to scratch the surface I discovered that under the current cover of Catholicism were the ancient pagan rituals simply disguised by Catholic symbolism.

Huachuma shamanism is a traditional form of pre-Incan healing still present in the Andes, in isolated villages and areas of Peru, Bolivia and Ecuador, mixed with various religious influences (especially Catholicism). The daily life of the inhabitants of these areas is full of mystical temples, sacred sites and unusual events (places of power, apparitions, ghosts, UFOs looked upon as spirits, etc). The methods of healing and of spiritual development associated with Huachuma shamanism refer to concrete experiences rather than to a religion, a philosophy or an alternative therapy. They constitute a way of life, a way of healing exploring our four dimensions: body, mind, emotions and spirit.

∞

I believe we live in an era of destruction of everything that is sacred. The heart of Mother Earth is heavy. The water, the mountains, the

air, the forests and the soul of *Pachamama* are polluted with ignorance, greed and arrogance. However, sacred wisdoms in the heart
of Mother Earth have been preserved here or there. This is the case
of Huachuma shamanism that has for a long time been part of the
reality for the inhabitants of the Andean mountains.

∞

After gaining an understanding of Huachuma shamanism, I
made the commitment to travel throughout the world to spread
the essence of this form of shamanism, in a simple way making
it possible for Westerners to incorporate these important prac-
tices into their everyday lives and which I will outline in the
following chapters.

# Songs

· · · · · · · · · · · · · · · · · · · · ☆ ☆ ☆ · · · · · · · · · · · · · · · · · · · ·

The Western world is full of sights, sounds, noises, colors and information. We are constantly bombarded with distractions of all kinds. In traditional communities sound is generally regarded as a very powerful expression of the essence of things. For me, a song of power (called an *icaro*) is the energy of an object expressed in sound with the true power becoming present in the intention behind the sound of the song.

From the shamanic perspective, when we start to listen to the cycles of our own body and of Nature we understand that the *icaros* come directly from Mother Earth, that silence does not exist, that sound is an essential part of the energy present in all life. The movement of energy creates a vibration that we can sometimes hear as a sound but that we may also not hear, because the scale of sounds is beyond our power of listening. Similarly, the incantations (the *icaros*) are at the same time audible and inaudible sounds for humans. This is why the chanting of a shaman may seem strange for Westerners (at least at the beginning). But, everything considered, is it not the noises that we hear in the "civilized" world which are very strange? The engines of cars, vacuum cleaners and washing machines, the squeaking of tyres, the ringing of telephones and fax machines, the buzzing of electricity, the crackling of lights, etc. All of these harmful and polluting noises that constantly surround us (without us always being aware of them) are not only irritating but they also reduce the energy of the body to a very low level. Accustoming ourselves to life at this basic level, we forget the beauty of the pure and simple sounds of nature: the song of a bird, the whistle of the wind, the trickling of water, and the silence of the night.

Through its sound, an *icaro* can manifest an aspect of Nature because it has the same deep quality. Faced with such an unusual concept, for instance, that a majestic tree can produce a song, a Westerner could say: "The tree does not make sounds." But if we open our ears beyond the basic level of existence, we hear that not only the tree but also each thing alive sings a song with its Spirit. The shaman listens to these songs and, under appropriate conditions, is able to chant the Spirit of all things alive. This helps him to move points of imbalance in bodies from the basic level towards the harmony that exists in Mother Earth.

The *icaro* is a vibratory bridge of energy for all beings living on Mother Earth. Some plants have for instance the power to slow down the bleeding of a wound. By singing the *icaro* of these plants, the shaman uses their power to slow down the bleeding and heal the wound. In Easter Island and in Tahiti, where I spent some time doing spiritual work with Polynesians, I observed that the *icaros* used by the old ones had been transformed into movements, mainly of the hands. By placing the hands in specific positions, it was possible to reproduce the symbolism of the sound and to procure a change in people's energy centers. The movement of the hands in Polynesia is related to symbols very similar to those existing in Egypt and in some parts of South America. The symbol itself only has its full meaning if the shaman activates it, just as an *icaro* does not have power if it is chanted without a pure intention (see Chapter 'Willpower and Intention').

The ritual of the *icaro* is often carried out in sacred places where the air is pure, such as very high in the mountains, close to waterfalls or special rivers, or in the snow. These places have the power of the air and the wind, two essential elements in the process of letting go and of transformation. It is often in sacred places such as these that I do my healing work.

If somebody comes to me and complains about a strong pain in the stomach, I can begin my therapy work by singing the Song of the Snake, while breathing deeply at the level of the abdomen and with eyes closed, communicating to the Spirit of the Snake. This song is traditionally used to release the force of life that is in the energy centercenters. (In some cultures this life force is referred to as *kundalini*.) From a western therapeutic framework, chanting the Song of the Snake to heal may surprise some and convince them of the idea (which for a long time has been supported by some anthropologists) that the strange behaviour of the shaman is a kind of madness. In western societies, the snake is generally perceived as negative, but in reality, what is negative is the spirit creating this image, this illusion. The snake is a part of nature, just like us.

Whilst chanting the Song of the Snake, slowly, the Spirit of the Snake comes to me like an image and I start to feel my body changing, the Snake moving to some extent in each cell of my Being. By this time, I am the Snake and I can simply chant as if the Snake was chanting in me. The sound that I then produce is more than words; it is the expression or the sign of the Snake. My intention is not to replicate the sound made by a snake, but to allow the person being healed to pass from a state of suffering to a point where he can see that the suffering is self-created, as an energy reality which is neither in the spirit nor in the emotions. The vibration of the Song of the Snake allows a transformation within me that helps the life force to rise and move to the top of my head. The same applies to the person with whom I work. Through the power of this sound, it is easy to move the life force beyond the point of imbalance where the suffering manifested itself in the person's body.

Seeing, for instance, that the life force of the person is blocked in his stomach, unable to express itself, and affecting the physical body with stress and anxiety, my intention is simply to move the block (which is the imbalance expressed at the basic level) towards a place where it is not harmful anymore. I try to separate the suffering from the experience of the person and to understand the energy that creates this dynamic. The physical symptoms as such do not concern me as much as the foundations that give rise to the situation. For instance, I do not focus myself on anger itself but on the energy that feeds it. The shamanic work cannot change the situation if the patient remains on the "basic level of existence." The solution does not consist in giving him a remedy, which simply removes the pain, but in helping to change the causes of the disease.

When the shamans sing an *icaro*, they sing from the depth of their heart or their higher Self. The intention of the song does not come from the ego but from the heart of their Being and thereby from Nature itself. Thus, when I chant with the Spirit of a special plant to prepare a medicine with this plant, my intention is not formulated in terms of "I want this medicine to heal a specific disease" or "I want this medicine to get rid of this disease" because that would come from the ego. With the heart we understand that the essence of things is directed towards perfection, even if what is around this essence is not perfect. This is why, when we sing a song, we do it from this perfection, which is profoundly strengthening. A chant for a plant can thus help us to create a remedy. With a pure intention, we communicate from the deepest part of our heart with the Spirit of the plant. We approach it by chanting in the most beautiful way and by listening to the information coming from this plant. If we sing this way for a long time, we start to communicate with the Spirit of this plant and become one with it. We travel in another dimension and we understand the natural laws that surround this plant. Its essence can then appear in a human form like a beautiful woman dancing around the plant, full of colors and beauty. This woman can sing for us and explain to us that today is a good day to prepare a medicinal herb because it is the cycle of new moon. That can be the beginning of our vision. The more we sing, the more we experience the vision and the essence of things.

To understand the *icaro* it is necessary to understand our body, the way we breathe, the way we communicate, both with the external world and the inner world. If we observe our breathing very attentively, we realize that it fully expresses what we are at the present time. Without power, full of pity for oneself, one cannot sing an *icaro* because it is a song of power. The energy of the song will convey the pity for oneself rather than the power of the balance contained in the reality of Mother Earth. If our breath is insufficient and in some ways limited, the song will convey this limitation and it will simply be a human song. The first stage to sing an *icaro* consists in releasing the breath. Only a pure intention allows our breath to freely move like the wind. That may seem simple but becoming conscious of our patterns of breathing requires many years of practice.

In Huachuma shamanism there is a mini *icaro* to detoxify the liver. It is realized with the sound *aahh*. Very simply, it helps to open the breath. By practicing the sound *aahh* we can notice how we energetically retain toxins in our bodies. We become aware of how the jaws and the tension around the face create a mask that prevents the true *aahh* from being expressed. This true *aahh* can come to us at times when one says *aahh* spontaneously – without any thought. It is the correct way of making the simple sound of the *icaro*. This sound appears when the heart is at peace with itself, when the spirit is focussed and when the emotions are fully expressed. It is particularly good to produce it when we are shocked or when we feel that fear is holding us back in our life. (To respect the body it is also important to respect the liver in the body.) With the chanting of this *icaro,* the *aahh* sound moves the blocked energy out of the liver helping it to detoxify. We are then able to move beyond the block where the shock and fear limit us. We can then live without fear, remove the trauma from our body and allow the power of the Cosmos, the harmony of Nature, to re-enter into this area of our physical being, allowing the healing to slowly affect our mental and emotional aspects as well.

Let us sing the pure and simple power of life and celebrate its plants, animals, color, movement and beauty. Let us enjoy the essence of things through the power of songs, building the bridge for us all (young and old) to experience the wondrous Universe that sings through our hearts.

# Breathing

· · · · · · · · · · · · · · · · · · · ☆ ☆ ☆ · · · · · · · · · · · · · · · · · · ·

In Huachuma shamanism, correct breathing is considered as the source of balance in life. While breathing in, one experiences expansion, while exhaling contraction. Between the in-breath and the out-breath, if our consciousness is in harmony with the expansion and contraction of the Universe and of all life, we can experience illumination.

If we remember our first breath, the moment when we came into the world, we can understand the power contained in that moment. When the baby takes his first breath, the Spirit enters his physical body. The expansion of the in-breath puts him in touch with the emotions and the mind. With the interruption of the breath, the experience of the emotions stops. In that split second, the baby can say "yes" or "no" to life. If he says "no," he is not balanced with his own spirit. In the same way, when we breathe with an emotion, if we are not aware of it, the experience of this emotion will be reproduced with the second breathing, and so on... The emotion thus reinforced then manifests itself in the body. This process often continues for many years until adulthood. One breathes and, very often, one says "no" to life, but on a level so subtle that our ego is not aware of it.

To practice some techniques of complete breathing, even for only ten minutes each morning, allows for an understanding of what is breathing.

If you only have time to practice one breathing exercise I would suggest this powerful ancient deep breathing technique. Practice it for two weeks and the results will speak for themselves. Then, if you like, practice it for the rest of your life.

This exercise is best done in fresh air both in the morning and in the evening.

1. Stand up tall or sit straight becoming aware of your lower ribs and diaphragm. Feel your hands totally relaxed. Join together your thumb and index fingertips on both hands and squeeze gently.
2. Take in a slow deep breath through your nose, making sure you feel the lower ribs and diaphragm expand and move outwards.
3. When you have filled your lungs and diaphragm with as much air as possible force yourself to breathe in more, so that your body is expanded to the maximum.
4. Now let the air out slowly through your mouth, keeping your lips partly closed so that a wind-like sound is audible throughout the complete exhalation of the breath.
5. When you have breathed out all of the air, suck in the lower ribs and diaphragm so that you are contracted to the maximum.

Do this exercise 5-7 times in a quiet space.

Breathing correctly is to say "yes" to life, to all the aspects of our self – the good and the bad. It gives us the courage to experience a part of ourselves that has been put aside for a very long time. There is no "short cut" for changing our breathing patterns or for entering into a harmonious relationship with the expansion and contraction of Mother Earth. It just requires practice, a practice that is not secret but requires time and discipline.

∞

When we are engaged in inner transformation, our tastes and the way we feel and see things change, just as the snake sloughs off its old skin thus allowing the new one to appear. We then realize just how much our breathing is connected to everything. Shallow/short and disjointed breathing expresses our weaknesses and our fears. We thus need to direct our efforts towards the development of a fuller and deeper way of breathing. Energy, particularly present in the lower zones of the body, starts to spread out and our experience of life becomes more intense, more brilliant. In dreams one can see the process of transformation like a part of oneself, as if in a granite (the rock which retains ancestral memories) cave. We could suddenly find in this cave an opening, which leads us to a treasure trove full of glistening gold and shining jewels.

Knowledge does not come from limitations but from freeing ourselves from our limitations. If our breathing is tainted with negativity, true knowledge cannot reach us because we limit ourselves. Through anger, depression or unhappiness, we become locked up in an illusion created by ourselves, thus separating us from the joy and happiness, which are the emotions at the deepest part of our Being. We reach Unity by transcending our limitations rather than transforming or destroying them. To go beyond these limitations, we can place ourselves in front of a mirror for a few minutes, observing our position, our lungs, our abdomen, our shoulders, and our self as they appear in the mirror. Are we breathing deeply? Breathing deeply into this moment is the easiest way to honor Life and our essence. By doing so, we start to say, "yes" to Life and begin becoming free in our body.

This state, which connects us with the essence of things, is impossible to acquire if, like most people, we have a pattern of shallow and disjointed breathing. This happens when the physical and energy body have incarnated fear and are separated from Love, from the flow of Life. In this situation, the breath changes its rhythm and is shortened. Our posture and our body energy are also maintained in fear and have an energy that attracts negative situations, even if it is only one reality created through the illusion of our thoughts. This type of shallow breathing pattern unconsciously expresses our separation from the idea that Life is perfect and not limited. Reality cannot then be experienced in its totality.

It is fascinating to see how, while saying, "yes" to Life, our health improves, our intelligence receives flashes of illumination, and our heartbeat slows down. The deceleration of the cardiac pulsations through breathing helps to oxygenate our blood and to release our muscles and our organs, which extends our life and allows us to appreciate the simple things of the world. It is a source of well-being and joyfulness in the spiritual and emotional domains as well as in the depths our Being.

While being attentive to our breathing, we understand that inner transformation has its foundations in the body and that deep, released, complete, natural breathing is a bond with parts of ourselves that are separated from Life and that must find harmonious balance with the power of Mother Earth. This is intelligence. Being angry, full of hate, committing suicide or blaming others for our problems leads nowhere. Not only do we destroy ourselves, but we also provide discomfort and suffering to others. By positively changing the rhythm and the depth of our breathing we can change our appearance and our consciousness. We can transform our anger and anxiety and we can stop damaging our body because we say, "yes" to Life.

As with the baby, everything begins with the breath. To breathe consciously in the present reminds us that each moment is an experience of freedom. Freedom is not acquired with a technique but is rather the expression of what we are physically and mentally. Each time we become aware of our breathing, let us place our Self in this moment. Let us release the body. Let us fill it with a deep, complete breath and let go, let go, really let go and let us be simply there, present to each wondrous moment. Deep, slow breathing is a breathing that fully expresses freedom.

# Willpower and Intention

Most people are driven by their willpower. Generally we do things in our lives because our will, our ego, creates the logic of: "I want this," "I want that," "When I have this... I will be happy; I will not suffer any more." But the will shows us the world in a way separate from how it really is. The "I want" syndrome creates patterns which can form a vicious circle of jealousy, anger and darkness, creating a world of fear, doubt and discomfort, moving us away from the true Self which is connected to Joy, Love and Light. In this world we see things from a very individual perspective that places a continual state of stress on our body, our breathing and our mind. We do not realize what motivates these "I wants." By having thoughts like "If I do not work I will not be able to pay my rent," or "if I do not do enough I will not be rewarded," we forget that the "I" is only an illusion and that this vicious circle will simply never satisfy us.

The emotional and mental fear, rooted in the body and the mind, may seem real to us but it is only an illusion as it is part of the unreal "I." This way of seeing can be found in the fear of becoming old, of remaining alone, of dying. This not only creates an uneasy feeling of separation, but it also profoundly supports the appearance of physical and mental diseases, states of thinness or obesity, asthma or bronchitis, problems of sight, etc.

Contrary to willpower, which brings into play the ego, intention is animated by the heart and our inner being. It is simply an expression of the pure love we have for all things and for all people. Its reference is not the past or future rather a deep presence to the fullness of life itself. When the ego does not have anything to want, there is no more situation of stress. When there is pure intention, the mind, the body and the breath are released. The more this intention relaxes us, the more we are present to the pure joy and happiness which is a part of all Life and which we should not be seeking outside of ourselves. In Huachuma communities, living life with pure intention is a way of behaving which borrows from the rhythms of Nature.

When shamans conduct their healing ceremonies, they place themselves in a space of pure Love, Joy and Happiness and by doing so ensure that their intention is pure. From this space, they offer gifts and offerings to Mother Earth and to all forms of life demonstrating the respect and connection they have with all that surrounds them. Their offering is not a prayer but rather an expression of their intention. In extending our Being into the present dynamics of life we escape the image of reality created by the ego and strengthen our awareness of life rather than yearning for everything. We participate as part of the Universe rather than from a space of desire.

∞

To describe the experience of such a healing ceremony with words is very difficult. To allow Life to help us understand the image of reality that we have created for ourselves, we must surrender ourselves to the energy of the Universe rather than that of the "I want" ego. This work requires real concentration at the beginning. It is about putting aside the games of the mind and the emotions and remaining connected to what is presented during the Ceremony, which is not easy. A good way to stay present is to be relaxed, doing nothing but simply remembering to breathe deeply and slowly (exhaling deeply on the out-breath). The more we breathe deeply and slowly the more we are connected with the present moment and with what surrounds us and are, thereby, more conscious.

Shallow, disjointed breathing, only in the higher part of the lungs, is the physical expression that we live out of our intellect and ego. This type of breathing testifies that we want to forcefully change or challenge things around us; that we want to change the built image of our life rather than to let go of it and connect to Mother Earth and the natural flow of life. Similarly, if we only breathe in the lower part of the lungs, on the level of the abdomen, we recognize the existence of our feelings. But that is certainly not enough. One can only really work with one's feelings and emotions when breathing with pure intention grounded and focussed in the heart. Even then it is not just our feelings but also our intellect and our physical being which must be centered in a space that is inspired by the harmonious rhythm of life. Full, complete breathing is realized when the lower, middle and higher parts of the lungs are all utilized in harmony. By changing our way of breathing, to that of full, complete breathing we can change our patterns of life. This requires effort.

∞

The secret of intention is also in our ability to communicate with Nature with a deeply relaxed body, with the breath full and total. Then we are able to sing songs that come naturally from the deepest part of ourselves and, through them, we can connect with subtle vibrations present in the Universe. This naturally opens our heart to express itself through sacred sounds.

∞

The cells of the body carry memories inside them and every cell in our body must support the intention. If the cells carry remnants of disharmonious feelings and memories they will color the purity of the intention. Centered on the divine and on perfection, intention focussed in the heart, can make all of our disharmonious thoughts and diseases disappear, but the process is slow and gradual as we truly become more present to ourselves. This is why, in Huachuma tradition, a ceremony can only be carried out by someone who has a pure intention. If our gift to Mother Earth is not an extension of our Self but rather an image of the daily reality that we are trying to change, then the ceremony will not have any magic or power. When the ceremony is conducted only with the power of the will (that of the ego), on some level, it will always convey some kind of negativity. The present will not be respected because the mind will be focussed on the past or the future and the images of the reality it has created.

The modern world created materialism in all aspects of life – in politics, science, and medicine. This limitation, endorsed by people, has become a reality they face and which constitutes a challenge for them: a will-driven collective. It prevents them from understanding the power of the Universe and seeing that the process of life is much more complex than it appears to be. For the shamans, the Western world now lives in the illusion they created, an illusion coming from the fact that they allowed themselves to be limited.

In contrast to this, a state of non-separation intensifies our feelings, reminding us of the primordial state of humankind and the amazing potential inherent in us all.

∞

When we sit down, let us be conscious of our breathing, conscious of any disharmonious thoughts and memories, conscious of the tensions in our body. Let us become aware of the images of reality we have created and let us see what happens when this consciousness is changed and we reach a state without any tension, a state of deep breathing focused on the heart, full of peace and deep stillness. Let us be aware of the process and the way in which all that seems impossible to us – because of the limitations we convey - may change and become possible. We then start to understand what intention is and the magic feeling that everything is possible appears.

# Separation

As children grow they hide parts of themselves. Indeed, at around seven months, the ego begins to settle into the child. The fontanel closes itself. The teeth (symbols of the ego) appear and a feeling of separation takes place. Adults, through various means, who have internalised this feeling of separation, might then involve themselves in the outside world with the acquisition of cars and material wealth, the consumption of drugs, the search for entertainments and excitations of all kinds. They should, for the oneness that they seek, do none of the above because what they are seeking is actually inside, not outside of themselves.

The inner world of a little child who painfully cries, hits out, bites and in other ways is naughty and destructive in his attempt to bring adult awareness towards his suffering can be compared to that of the above wounded adult. Unless the child's fear of separation is recognised, is honestly talked about and consciously transformed by the loving actions and consistent examples of his parents, the child and the adult will both continue to run away from parts of themselves, creating frustration and disease on many levels of their lives.

The compulsion to find the perfect partner, to buy the red Ferrari, to earn a lot of money, comes from an inner world which is in darkness but which is endeavoring to reach the light. The energy of this dark inside world needs to be consciously recognised and honored. If it remains locked up in the small existential box that it has manufactured, made up of limitations, separations, suffering and fear, it will continue to express itself in a negative and destructive way.

I believe that this separation is the driving force behind wars, family feuds and other personal and marital conflicts.

What is the solution? Conflict resolution must start by stilling the internal conflicts within oneself rather than trying to change the external world. Today, more than ever we must be able to embrace the principle that shamanic and traditional societies value dearly – that everyone and every living part of Nature is connected and is to be honored in every moment as one would honor a special guest.

The following simple exercise is a powerful way to remind ourselves of love. Each small step we take along the path to oneness creates great impact on those around us, which may not be obvious immediately, but is obvious nonetheless in the higher realms and in the deepest parts of our hearts.

*Find a comfortable, quiet space and sit or lie down in readiness for the exercise.*

Breathe deeply into the area of your heart. Slowly breathe in and slowly breathe out. As you breathe out let go of your frustration, stress and anger. Imagine and feel the presence of the person you love most, coming towards you smiling and extending their hands out as if to embrace you. Feel the love and warm sensations that you have towards them as you smile back and reach out to embrace them.

Now begin to visualise that this person changes into the person that you would most like to resolve a conflict with. See them smiling at you in the same loving way and open your heart as you did with the person you most love. Remember not to allow yourself to go back to the negative thoughts or feelings this person may invoke in you. Instead, all the time, open your heart to the feelings you have for the person you most love (do this a few times if this is difficult) and continue to return to the image of the person you want to resolve the conflict with.

You will be surprised that the heart will find this easy but the mind (ego) will try to sabotage your efforts. As soon as you are successful in bypassing this sabotage your chosen person of resolution will have a bridge of change open to them as you have changed your image of this person within yourself.

Through this exercise you will learn that change begins within and that the outside world follows suit accordingly.

# Freedom

· · · · · · · · · · · · · · · · · · ☆ ☆ ☆ · · · · · · · · · · · · · · · · · · · ·

Shamanism, as old and mystical as it is, may be re-appropri-ated and practiced by Westerners in their everyday life and may constitute a new way of life based on ancestral wisdoms. Our ancestors understood that freedom is based on fitting into a Cosmos where all is One and where the One carries an expression of all. With the rapid polarisation of the modern world into ego driven desires and conflicts, from a self orientated towards itself, we have lost this sense of balance and are in great danger of living in a selfish world, which moves away from Life. Now, more than ever, it is important to create a bond between the deep balance of Nature that is the essence of Life and our daily activities. In the future, this balance will probably become more common in the economy, philosophy, politics and the general thinking of Western societies, as more and more people practice spiritual disciplines oriented towards the realization of this harmonious goal. Humanity will be always preferred to death, just like freedom will always be preferred to limitation.

What makes Huachuma shamanism so special is that it considers freedom as a gift of Nature and the Cosmos to mankind? One can fully experience freedom as a gift when one perceives life through the conscious inner Self. Spiritual work is about understanding and going beyond the negative forces that prevent us from saying, "yes" to Life. These forces are actually a manifestation of imbalance. The choice then is do we live according to the forces of imbalance, creating disharmony inside and around us, or do we create a balance in our lives, by living in harmonious relationship with natural and cosmic forces, which is what shamanism is about. This is what our ancestors did and what some people in traditional societies still do today with much less distraction than in the modern world.

When we start to abandon our everyday life distractions and we become conscious of the forces of imbalance, which affect our deep Self, a question emerges completely naturally: "Until when will we allow these forces to disturb our balance?" All is a matter of choice and expression of our freedom. Making the good choice allows us to go beyond what causes limitation in our life. And if from the deepest part of the Self we understand that the limitation is a creation based on a simple thought, we can then use this thought – as limited as is it – to reinforce our intention to turn us to the present rather than to the past. Being present to our body, our mind and our emotions gives the freedom to experience Joy and Love. This freedom expresses the inner Self in a very creative way.

The experience that consists of finding Totality or Unity in our lives is the true significance of Love. We can be dissatisfied when this Joy and Love do not animate us and do not surround us, when we feel that reality is made up of violence, poverty, disease and wounded souls. In Huachuma shamanism, these things are not reality but rather thoughts that create our experience. Life has decided these things for us but we always have the choice to avoid being internally disturbed by the external circumstances. We can, for example, decide not to be moved by praises or criticisms. We can assume responsibility for our actions and refuse to consider ourselves as a victim. A choice of this nature changes everything.

Each thing has its place in the world, even suffering. If we accept it as a part of ALL that IS, the suffering becomes an opportunity to free ourselves from negativity. It can magically be transformed to become an experience of Totality or Union. Suffering is a gift of Nature because it is the law that prevents the Universe from collapsing, the law that maintains the unity of the Cosmos. This law of balance appears everywhere and also in every human being. The only problem is that the mind and the ego, that distinguish humans from other living beings, prevent them from experiencing this balance.

When the mind and the ego make the distinction of the external world as separate from oneself, they create a complex of thoughts and feelings that produce a system of beliefs. They then only answer to external situations without being able to make a choice, without the freedom to see beyond the illusion of the separation they have created. Circumstances come and go, but the external determinant persists and, day after day, is reinforced. Because of the feeling of lacking freedom, they end up running after things considered as conveying joy and constantly experience great discomfort. Some think that through the control of this or that with more money, more health, more protection against the hurts and violence, that their lives could be merrier. And maybe they are for a brief moment but then circumstances change again and again and to experience happiness, we continue our search for joy while trying to change the external world. We think that by detaching ourselves from the suffering we will be happy. But the realization of these desires does not bring happiness because it is based on an avoidance of Life.

The more we try to control the world that surrounds us, the less we have freedom. The discomfort we feel results from the resistance to know the truth and in the belief that the mind and the ego, which express separation, can understand Totality and Union. However, Joy and Peace come from Union and Totality. They are not external to us but are rather an integral part of ourselves and an extension of all that we do. True freedom comes from the inside, which does not know separation.

As soon as we recognize that the mind and the ego do not offer satisfactory solutions to our quest for Happiness, for Love, for Joy, for Peace and for Spirituality, and that any fight, any research and any waiting for something separate and outside of ourselves are a waste of time, then we can experience freedom. To let go of this belief is really magical. One calms down quite naturally and in this peace one can be in touch with Totality. Like the Phoenix rising out of the ashes, a new attitude emerges for life. A comprehension is formed in our hearts. We can reorient our beliefs and create a foundation for freedom and transformation. This place of understanding from which we feel comfortable in all circumstances comes from inner peace rather than from waiting or researching anything. Then each step we take on our path naturally becomes an expression of Freedom, Joy and Love. Loneliness, if it occurs, does not cause sadness any more as our needs are no longer determined by the external world. We do not need to fill up our life with this or that.

Happiness is quite naturally present in the deep experience of non-separation. One then understands that it is not necessary anymore to focus ones life on the outside, to separate from the world, to hide in a cave, inaccessible to Life. Quite the contrary, it is a matter of being deeply united with the world, of experiencing Life in all of its totality - of opening oneself to situations and to circumstances in a balanced way, in order to feel calmer, more at peace.

Happiness in its purest form brings light and awareness to all of the shades of discomfort. Our consciousness slowly moves in a direction where all becomes a part of it, all becomes lighter. It is a gradual process where space and energy arise in two basic forms: expansion and contraction. In Huachuma shamanism, the consciousness of breathing reflects a fundamental law of the Universe. We know that, through the inspiration of our breath we experience expansion, and through the expiration we experience contraction. But it is important to realise that the universe and all creation are also experiencing expansion and contraction. The awareness that the Universe and all Creation are in a continuous process in which we are included requires a deep quietude inside.

Trapped by external imbalance, we live in the shade of the night, forgetting that the darkness and the suffering are simply expressions of an incomplete bond depriving us from the freedom to realize our unlimited potential; depriving us from experiencing Joy. But, the more we raise the level of our consciousness with the idea of the interconnection of each thing, the more deeply we experience wellbeing and spiritual vitality.

To have an inside quest with the intention of adjusting oneself to the order of things helps to create a feeling of trust; providing a deep respect for oneself and the world. Imagine becoming still, quite naturally, and, in this stillness finding wholeness. What a marvellous feeling to be in harmonious relationship with All that Is - a feeling of right participation in the Universe.

# The Four Directions and the *Mesa*

In most ancient and native societies around the world, the four directions are fundamental signposts, with each giving a particular comprehension of the complexity of the cosmos. Huachuma shamanism sees the Universe and the world we live in as a large cobweb, whose various parts are interconnected while being separate. The Universe is considered as a part of each human Being, and vice versa and whilst connecting to it, one allows oneself to transform.

Personal transformation consists in giving up the easy ways, in letting go of the world we have created, to reach a state of detachment or "non responsibility." Responsibility is a form of control. To develop a state of "non responsibility" is to remove the need to stick to things as they are or to control them, which implies a major transformation within us.

This transformation means to take life seriously and realise its preciousness. Instead of simply playing the game of life, with the implicit suffering related to this play, one can put oneself aside and deeply look at why things are as they are. This however usually does not occur as long as a situation giving meaning to life does not touch us. It can be a painful crisis that shatters our existence but it can also help us to realize that there is much more to Life than the small worlds in which we live and perhaps in which we take pleasure. Of course, this realization, which puts aside the ego, can be terribly painful. Awareness often arises from pain. The first step consists in going beyond the illusion we have created for ourselves, that is to let go and develop a higher state of consciousness. To help us in the development of this consciousness, the Huachuma shamans work with the *mesa* and the four directions.

The *mesa*, or medicine wheel, is a sacred space made up of interrelated symbols. The shaman often places a ruby or other special crystals and stones in the center of the *mesa*, as well as statues, sacred temple items and amulets of jaguars and other animals, to call upon the Spirits of Mother Earth. He sees this space as an altar that helps us focus more clearly on the natural laws, which may assist us to find balance inside ourselves. Used in a traditional way, the *mesa* allows the change to be harmoniously carried out inside the parameters of the four cardinal points, thus determining our place in the Cosmos and helping us expand our awareness of the interconnectedness of all life. Each direction represents some different energies of life, in association with different totem animals, plants, rocks and other inherent qualities of Nature.

Although each culture assigns specific meanings to the four cardinal points, their basic connotations are universal. Everywhere in the world, people have directed their lives and their communities according to the four directions, the skies and the earth:

- South is the direction of activity, movement, heat, growth, the wind and letting go. Reptiles, such as the snake, the lizard or the crocodile, often represent it.
- North is the direction of peace, the black hole, cold, inner retrospection, the psyche and water. The owl or the dragon often represent it.
- East is the direction of the rising sun that symbolizes new beginnings, illumination, birth and rebirth, visions, the

awakening of consciousness, the body and the earth. The condor, the eagle or the hawk often represent it.

- West is the direction of the sunset, reflection, contemplation, relaxation, the reordering of things, forgiveness, fire, death, light, oneness, the blood, the essence, the Being and the heart. The jaguar, the lion or the Phoenix often represent it.

The significance of the four cardinal points is highly practical and provides a basis for putting our daily cycle of activities in relation to the cycles of the sun, to provide a sense of rightful participation in the Universe. To follow the significant planetary movements, our ancestors set up stones in circles, temples and sacred spaces. Today, we can re-explore these relationships and understand our place in the web of Life.

∞

I will now describe in-depth the meanings associated with the direction South and North and, more briefly, those associated with the directions East and West. This will allow the reader the opportunity of exploring him or herself.

## South

The South allows us to let go of our past and the energy connected to it. In this direction we release the emotions that, in the body, are often localized in the lungs, according to the way we breathe. Associated with the element air and the Spirit of the Wind, the south helps us to understand that what we think as permanent is actually impermanent. More than a physical direction, the South is also a part of our body, our mind and our emotions.

The way in which we see the world is often that which was developed during the first eighteen months of our life. If we suffered from a trauma in childhood, or later in life, it is in this direction that this trauma is stored, and it is there that the element wind is blocked. Our concepts of the world are often formed through negative experiences, even traumatic ones that do not allow us to go further in our representation of things. Ideas and images from the worldly environment are also printed on the body and, through time, are reinforced. A particular image of reality, an illusory image among many other possible, then determines the experiences of life and their interpretations. The wind is blocked. Energy does not flow. But it is not necessary to store the suffering in this direction eternally. When the Huachuma shaman addresses the Spirit of the Wind, he can ask him to help make the trauma disappear. The Wind allows the movement of energy and helps nature to be expressed in a more balanced and flowing way.

For the shaman who works in the direction South, it is not necessary to analyze or understand the world through a particular image of reality. Rather, he will sing an *icaro* like the Song of the Snake. The snake is a favourite totem animal in this direction and represents the movements of energy. By helping us to give up the need to control things, it allows a process of transformation to take place. By singing this song, the shaman gives power to the part of the body associated with the Snake. In doing so, he helps this sick part engage in the process of letting go. Letting go of the feelings, the built images, the memory and the ideas stored in the body allows the patient to start seeing things in a different way. His attachment to the old images of reality that limited him transforms itself into attachment with living Nature. The relationship to Life and presence is recreated. With the Song of the Snake, the shaman asks Mother Earth, to take part in this transformation.

∞

Often, the shaman communicates with plants, which are connected to the South to know how to heal a given disease. The plants associated with this direction are strongly related to the wind, for example corn, whose energy of life is related to this element, in contrast with potatoes, whose energy is much more terrestrial (the corn grows upward towards the wind, the potato grows downward towards the earth). Observing the processes concerned with the plants in this direction can help inform us about the process, which is taking place within us and support our development of balance and harmony.

Sometimes, I use a flower-remedy strongly associated with the South and its characteristics of movement and growth. This particular remedy gently helps us to go beyond inside blocks, which prevent us from being in balance with this direction. In a powerful but subtle way, it helps us to let go. One day I gave drops of this sensitive plant (which retracts when it is touched) to an Australian woman. This woman had always been extremely closed about her past, even that of her own family. Suddenly, it came back to her memory and she started to talk about things she was not aware of before, which strongly embarrassed her. She said to me later that while listening to herself talking she wondered whether it was really her who spoke. The intelligence of the Plant, its Spirit, had helped this woman understand the direction South and to move her emotions blocked for many years and which had caused many problems in her life. The nature of this very beautiful medicine is its movement.

In the direction South we often work with our fears and irritations. The most sensitive zones of our bodies that express these feelings are the nose, the eyes and the ears. Blocked energies are normally expressed in these openings. If a person suffers from allergies, which become particularly strong when the wind carries pollen, or if he has problems with breathing, or if he wears glasses, this means that he has problems in the direction South. More specifically with letting go, and perhaps he needs care in handling his imbalance in this direction. If a person is hearing badly or has a problem with the ear, what he cannot listen to is often the truth behind the image that he created of himself.

∞

In complete balance with each direction, the shaman does not need to use his mind or his intellect. He intuitively knows when there is an imbalance. The way in which a person breathes, the movement of his lungs, the connection between his breathing and the mobility of his body often give a clearer idea of his disease and suffering than mere intellectual analysis.

If someone comes to me with a wart on his or her body and tells me they are very happy, I observe that their breathing is not harmonious and therefore their happiness is superficial. They are trying to hide a problem, to detach themselves from it with the result that they breathe badly using only the upper part of the lungs so as to avoid facing their true feelings. The wart is simply an expression of this block and, in this direction it is not at all negative. It is a friend saying to the person with the wart: "See what you are doing, let go and allow energy to move, to flow and to settle in your stomach." But because they are afraid of what is expressed by the wart, it remains a poignant reminder. They want to be unaware of it, they try to get rid of it, which is in fact impossible because, as the shamans see it, all is inter-connected in the world.

Fear is a feeling, or more exactly a lack of feeling, which reinforces this image that we believe to be reality. It is an energy that prevents us from going forward but we are not aware of it. Working with this process is a little like peeling an onion: the more we create harmony in this direction, the more we approach our essence, the more energy moves and the less things there are on which to cling.

Blocks in the direction South are localized in the first chakra, where fear and resentment tend to be placed. It is only when we start to let go that this energy can rise. And when we let go of the negative image that created our reality, then we can we see the world as it is, even our dreams start to change. As soon as we embrace life without fear and resentment, the dark colors, often present in dreams, transform into lighter colors.

By making friends with the "monsters" of our dreams, we realize that they are actually "friends". This is why in temples, the drawings or representations of monsters (which are, of course, really only other aspects of ourselves which we haven't acknowledged) were often honored. Rather than pushing them back, the shaman considers them important in order to understand the obscure dimensions within us. In the ancient temples, one often sees snakes associated with our ancestors, carved in rocks similar to granite (which is very dense and heavy) as they have the power to store subtle energy information. If we are attentive, we understand that these vestiges of our ancestors are elements of our evolution.

In the direction South, we have two possibilities: to go further or to interpret the world through a negative image, which means to regress into the darker, stagnant parts of ourselves. To go further requires courage, which we often lack when we live in fear.

If our ancestors and our families have lived in a world or a culture of fear, it can be difficult to face it and to go forward. In this direction, we must not only let go of our own psychological fears but also our cultural and ancestral ones. The energy of these fears is localized in the back of the brain, in the brain known as the "reptilian" or "primary brain." Harmonious intention, as the opposite of fear, conveys the power of the Wind - of freedom and movement - and we can create an internal experience of it through breathing. As I already mentioned, intention is a state of "non responsibility" or non-attachment, a place of deep releasing, where we allow the essence of Life to create a real image, not generated by fear.

It is probably in the direction South that many Westerners, accustomed to some obsessive patterns of restrictive behaviors (cigarettes, alcohol, drugs, etc), must work the most. We only have to look around us to note that, acting upon the reptilian brain, the majority of people are centered on materialism. This dependence rises largely from the human belief in their own power, which they place above the power of creation. While sticking to the will of desire, their ego-self becomes a slave to materialism, which weakens their connection with Nature, the fundamental element of Life. Cigarettes, alcohol, money, family or anything, are only an expression of the reality we live in, a reality where the limitations are created by the ego, which hopelessly seeks to enter into relationship with something. Working in the direction South we realize that the ego finally has no power and that our life is marked by an absence of connection to anything. The real power comes to us from a balanced relationship with ourselves and with what surrounds us. To let go of these old patterns that create our limitations, inevitably increases the power of our body, our mind and our soul.

To let go of the "I cannot" and its world of limitations, the shamans ask Mother Earth to help them. The Snake, seen as the energy of Life, is a good friend to have here also. When I sing the Song of the Snake, I call upon the power of this animal to work on the limitations of "I cannot." I go beyond the Song of the Snake and listen to the vibration of the "I cannot" – to all of the subtleties the self creates in order to justify its existence. When it becomes obvious, I help to change it into "I can." This allows changing the structure of the thoughts and all aspects in the body and the spirit creating these blockages.

It is noticeable when people start to feel very heavy and tired, when a part of them says, "I prefer not to change, it is too difficult," that the spiritual mastery of the shaman is essential. To go from one level of consciousness to another requires a lot of energy. This is why the shaman brings the abundant energy of Mother Earth into the process of transformation to enable reaching a healthier and higher level of consciousness. Free, without limitation, one moves towards the light.

This process of transformation needs to be rooted in reality. It is here that the ego can reappear in the situation carrying remnants of the old limitations with it. One can thus start to think in a negative way: "Did I really change?" "Can I change?" "Is this only an illusion?" Our reality at this time is simply one of doubt, with ideas like: "I cannot," "I doubt," or "I need more evidence" etc. This doubt reduces energy in the base chakra, which in turn can generate a myriad of problems in our lives. Yet, without fully knowing it, we have moved towards a higher level of consciousness, even if the doubt in our spirit can make us still feel caught in limitations. The Song of the Snake has reached the most obstinate part of the mind, the reptilian brain, and it has led to the emergence of an inner process moving the energy-power from the base chakra towards the solar plexus, an essential zone of letting go.

How does the shaman work to transform the doubt into a better comprehension of "I can" and "I realize" in daily reality? What does he do to break the habit of the mind, the body and the emotions, which carry this limitation? He confronts the doubt and works with it on the level where the suffering and doubt are. Then he symbolically extracts the doubt and suffering from the solar plexus by bringing these dynamics to the surface, not only on an emotional level but also on the fundamental level which creates one's general vision, or perceptions of life. The person can then understand the tricks of the mind in a symbolic but wonderfully clear way.

At this stage, the *mesa* becomes very important. Generally the shaman will take an invisible sword from the *mesa* that represents the transformation of the player of tricks into a warrior. With the sword, he cuts the energy feeding the doubt. He can then take various other swords, each representing a deeper aspect of the releasing. In a symbolic way the shaman becomes the "trickster of the mind," allowing the blocked situation to become obvious. He then evolves as a warrior to transform the doubt of the person he is working with so that she finds her existential reality, her deep Self, a free Self, full of health and unencumbered by the old destructive programming.

Respect, being essential in this work, the shaman may also sing a special song, specifically for the objects placed on the *mesa* calling upon their power. Then the shaman honors in particular the part of the body of the person with whom he works while placing a gift in the direction South on the *mesa*. The gifts to Mother Earth can take the shape of corn, tobacco, or any plant considered as sacred in the culture, to introduce the harmony and balance of Mother Earth into this new situation. What the shaman can do everybody can do but we often prefer not to do it, or not know how to do it.

∞

It can be interesting to remember that the moment when our teeth appear, generally at around six or seven months old, is the moment when the reptilian brain wakes up to the energy centers of the body and when the ego appears. During the following twelve months the brain develops itself very quickly. We start to construct basic ideas about the world and our centers of energy (or chakras) develop accordingly. If one faces limitations during these eighteen months, one will build a basic idea containing an energetic reality that continues to live in the reptilian brain and then becomes a natural way of seeing things. This energy affects each muscle and each cell of the face. It is particularly noticeable in the eyes, the ears, the nose and also the teeth.

During the process of reconnection and transformation of oneself, one does not only change at the emotional and spiritual level but also at the physical level. These changes become very obvious in the structure of the teeth – which become stronger, whiter – and of gums, even if the teeth are generally the last aspect of our physical body to change because they have a direct bond with the reptilian brain. The teeth constitute a solid structure of the patterns of energy and movement produced by the reptilian brain. This is why, all over the world, when, at around seven years old, children lose their baby teeth the event is ritualized. The learning of reality is consequently different, because this loss marks the passage to another reality. The magical dimension of the teeth is very important everywhere. The shaman can therefore have jaguar teeth on the *mesa* as an ultimate symbol of transformation.

## North

North is the direction of powerful magnetism. In this direction we are physically but also psychically inter-connected with things. Each thought, each action, each feeling has a psychic manifestation that all living beings can intercept. Babies and generally children below five years old are particularly vulnerable because they are able to see or feel these manifestations and to accept their reality. In certain areas of South America, the newborn is washed with special water to be protected from all such manifestations especially around certain phases of the moon. Also in this direction we can communicate with spirits and fairies around plants and trees.

Before eighteen months babies are like sponges absorbing everything which surrounds them and that affects the energy centers of their body. When the fontanel closes itself, the physical and psychic bodies become individualized and strengthened. The pituitary and pineal glands send specific messages to the glandular systems within the body. The energy inside the glands awakens, particularly in the thyroid gland (which is related to balance, communication, and the immune system). This protects the baby from the psychic residues (anger, inhibited feelings, etc). This gland is strongly dependent on the element water (also associated with the direction North), on rivers and any naturally flowing water. It helps us connect to the powerful cycles and natural rhythms of the various phases of the moon, the tides, and the biological rhythms of the body (like sleep and wake) that guide our senses, our emotions and our psyche.

When the shaman works in the direction North, he observes the stars and the seasons, and reads the natural signs in the sky to guide him in his work. Some animals like owls, wolves, frogs, turtles and dolphins help us connect with the water and the moon. The turtle is often looked upon as an animal that represents psychic knowledge and allows our unconscious Self to emerge from the depths. When one works with the psyche or the astral body, these animals can help to reconnect us with the natural cycles. Through these cycles, we realize that everything (lunar energy, animal energy, the wolf, the owl, etc.) is electrically charged and directly affects our pituitary and pineal glands. If the energies that animate us are in balance with the cycles of nature, these glands produce a special fluid that flows down to the thyroid, the area where the psychic body is protected. In contrast, the negative energies reduce and slow down the functions of the glands. I believe these energies flow to everywhere, as every thought, every action and every feeling has a psychic manifestation, which can be picked up by all living beings.

Babies increase the function of their pituitary and pineal glands naturally by putting the end of their tongue in contact with the higher part of their palate. This instinct helps them to manage and go beyond the situations of fear and sorrow, stress, discomfort, etc. We can do this for ourselves by singing an *icaro* called the Song of the Moon. The end of the tongue goes up to the top of the palate and creates a special sound; a vibration which allows the flow of fluid from the pituitary gland towards the thyroid. This song comes from the Amazon and is as follows:

*Ripi ripi ripi ripi ripi ripi ripi eia iah*

The power of this *icaro* is less in the sound itself than in the change of vibration that takes place at the top of the head, the neocortex. We are able to change this vibration so that it closely adjusts itself to that of the moon: the Spirit of the Moon then becomes to some extent a part of ourselves. This helps us to open our psyche in a way impossible with intellectual logic. During full moon, when the pituitary and pineal glands are more active, the unconscious rises up to the surface and, in doing so, reveals hidden psychic debris. This is one of the best times for the singing of this *icaro*.

The cycles of the moon strongly affect water, not only through the tides, but also through plants and our own bodies. Working with the power of the direction North in nature, the shaman can pour sacred water, infused with flowers coming from various parts of the mountains (which are regarded as charged with powerful magnetism), or perhaps on stones ceremoniously placed on the *mesa*, and then he will sing some *icaros* to reinforce these stones. He could use crystals, which in South America are regarded as pure water crystals and have the same characteristics and function as sacred water. These crystals are particularly powerful when they are placed under the full moon.

Water is perceived by the shaman as a manifestation of psychic influences; during times of particular psychic imbalances, the shaman might go to special places very high in the mountains, or to thermal sources, and bathe in the natural waters located there in order to purify the psychic energy around him and also to find balance with the harmonious cycles of Nature.

In Huachuma shamanism, thermal water is regarded as very sacred because it is full of positive ions and electromagnetic vibrations, qualities that help to put the pituitary and pineal glands directly under the influence of the moon and the sun. South American temples are often placed close to thermal sources, precisely for this reason.

There is an old tradition in the Andes where all the members of the village (men, women, old and young people), on a special day of the year, go to the top of their revered mountain to collect a little bit of ice or sacred snow. Then they bring it back down to the village and make a special ritual to purify the psychic environment of their community. This event usually takes place during the full moon and is accompanied by songs. For the villagers, ritual exists in order to remove residues from the past (as they physically and symbolically rise to the top of the mountain, the purest place of Mother Earth) and then, to purify the village with the positive energy contained in the ice and the snow, upon their return.

Indigenous populations of South America, more in balance with the subtle changes and cycles that take place around them, like the full moon, make special ceremonies to harmonize the psychic influences on the community. In contrast, in the West, these changes and cycles are often considered as moments when people and their behaviours are easily influenced in a negative way, resulting in an increase in the number of psychoses, fires, unusual accidents and other such events. Statistics indicate how much the full moon is affecting people: many feel sick, more anxious, and paranoid and/or have more obsessive behaviours. During this period, as the unconscious comes closer to the surface bringing with it hidden psychic debris, unless acknowledged in a positive way, there are also often more conflicts.

∞

The shaman sees energy as being in constant movement. He understands that it cannot be stopped but must always move, in cycles and according to the rhythms of Nature. Disease is thus considered as the expression of a pure and good energy that is blocked. It (the disease) expresses the life force that wants to solve an unhealthy blockage. Rather than try to counteract the disease, to push back this reality, the shaman endeavours to make the body able to manage it. When the disease appears in the physical body, the energy process slows down in its basic form, in the matter. However the disease is not only a physical problem, it also has a psychic origin. The shaman will place courage and power in the situation to enter more deeply into the energy process that takes place. To give a remedy that slows down this process even more, or expels it from the material dimension, (which is the result most prescription drugs have that remove the symptoms of disease but don't address the cause) is like deferring the problem to be solved later. To resolve the problem at the psychic level, the shaman's healing will on the contrary accelerate and reinforce the energy process, generally with the help of the natural rhythms of the moon and water. If psychic imbalance is not worked with and is not recognized on the psychic plane, it materializes itself in a physical form in a place previously healthy. The powerful magnetism of the direction North helps us to go beyond the psychic imbalance and debris that affect the physical body.

## East

While working with the direction East, we learn how to connect more completely to the Earth and its laws. We learn how to nourish ourselves internally, how to be at peace with ourselves, to be positively in deep relationship with the Earth and its Beings, particularly the world of plants. Majestic trees are a beautiful manifestation of the pure light towards which they rise.

The East is a creative process of transcendence in which the opposites (yin/yang; black/white, etc.) are united to produce a new positive phase. At the emotional and spiritual level, the sun rises in the East giving birth to light each new day after the hours of darkness.

The shamanic work in the direction East is very often achieved by the physical body being detoxified with some plants or herbs. The vomiting provoked by these plants allows the cleaning of the physical, emotional and spiritual bodies and releases their bonds that connect them to their karma and to the material power of the world.

Concretely, if the shaman works with somebody suffering from cancer, he will go beyond the material realm or the manifestation of cancer and will observe this disease from a spiritual standpoint. Rather than apprehend it like something bad to be afraid of, he will see it as forming part of the Totality that is important to recognize. He could sing an *icaro* that calls upon the Spirit of the Eagle and, while working with its help, he will see the aspects of cancer difficult to grasp in normal reality, and that need to be worked on at the emotional level.

The eagle, the condor and other birds of prey – creatures associated with the East – are very good friends to have in this direction. The shaman evokes these animals to ask them to fly like they do beyond the obstacles of the terrestrial existence in order to see things from a higher and radically different perspective. Traveling beyond the physical body, he can experience the disease, or more precisely, communicate with the Spirit of the Disease, to learn from it.

∞

In the Amazon, to facilitate the transitions related to the changes of consciousness, the shamans also use a plant called *Ayahuasca*. The word *Ayahuasca* comes from the Quechua language. *Aya* is the vibration that affects the liver and the solar plexus and helps open them. It also means death (as in death/rebirth). The sound *aya* means to let go of or to disconnect from things that imprison a person, in order to give rise to a new life in which things can be approached differently. *Huasca* is the path that leads us further (it is also the word for vine).

In the Andes, the shamans use another sacred plant called *Huachuma*, the name given to the shamanism we refer to here. *Huachuma* is made of two words: *hu* meaning "spirit" and *achuma* is that which occurs when this plant is taken, that is "getting closer to creation." The first sound of *achuma* is again *aahh* that opens the solar plexus and the liver in the same way towards the Spirit.

The cactus called *San Pedro*, used in ceremony with a guide, also helps to deal with certain aspects of the psyche and the Self. Drunk in decoction, it provides its power and its intelligence to help people to work through specific aspects within themselves. The positive and the nutritive nature of the world of plants and trees are obvious to those who open their heart to them. The plants help the solar plexus to connect to elements lighter and higher than the heaviness of the psychic residues and toxins that generally influence our life, teaching us how to more completely and more harmoniously connect to Mother Earth.

A certain number of specific physical exercises (See Chapter 'Energy Postures') are also associated with the East. They help us to let go of disease and to reconnect with Mother Earth. These ancient exercises are energy movements rather similar to yoga. They open the solar plexus and, very gently and subtly, work with the lower organs like the liver and the kidneys, to establish more harmonious and healthier vibrations. In the temples of northern Peru, they are often presented in the direction East. The postures in question can seem strange and contorted, but, when they are practiced, they open the body to an incredible energy of which most of us are not aware. Often after having practiced these exercises, people were buried for several hours in the argillaceous (clay-like) earth of certain areas of Peru to clean their skin and to allow the toxins and the negativity contained in their body to be physically and symbolically absorbed by Mother Earth.

# West

This direction is probably the most difficult to work with because it is the direction of death and rebirth. In the West we can understand that fear and death are not obstacles but rather transitions towards various levels of perception of the world. This direction is often better understood with the assistance of the jaguar or the lion. The lion has a symbolic nature that was always important for our ancestors. Like all the members of the cat family, it has a mysterious dimension. In ancient Egypt, the lion represented the living power of the sun, whose spiritual aspect was known under the name *Ra*. It was feared because of its great physical power but also respected as symbolizing the messenger of death and the after life. When it roars, death resonates. Even if we do not have a direct bond with the ancient Egyptian culture or the lion, the power of this symbol keeps the same depth in our unconscious. In European cultures, cats hold a similar position and are often feared and associated with witches, again because of the power, the unpredictability and the supernatural knowledge associated with them. The large felines of the Amazon hold a similar position in South America. During Ceremonies shamans can transform into jaguars which are considered the largest of all the cats and who howl in the jungle to keep people away from death and misfortune. The gleam of its eyes is likened to the last rays of the sun received into the hearts of animals. This interconnection with the jaguar gives the shaman even more power to understand death, misfortune and fear.

In the Andes, West is the direction where the shaman can experience illumination, that is the letting go of fear and the ideas that prevent him from being connected to the Great Spirit. In this direction, death is often experienced on a level both concrete and symbolic. The rebirth takes place when one feels unity within oneself and when this unity goes beyond the physical and spiritual fears of separation and death. Shamans often do exercises that directly bind them to the energy of the sun and this helps them to go beyond death, or to be as One with the Great Spirit.

∞

The healing Ceremonies normally take place in sacred spaces with thermal sources. The vapors are generally used to heat the body, particularly the blood, to allow transformation to occur. In other cultures, people used thermal or sacred water in places of power to help the body to transform through heat. The transformation of the thermal water into vapor was a way of helping the body to remember the transformation that takes place on the different and deeper levels of oneself. The sweat lodges of North American Indians and other cultures were also very important, not simply to detoxify the body but also to maintain a connection with the Great Spirit.

Very often in the Huachuma tradition, during a ceremony the shaman will place alcohol on the *mesa* and light a symbolic fire. (This would be at around three in the morning.) All of the elements of the *mesa* receive the energy of the fire, which gives more power to the work carried out in the Ceremony. The fire symbolically burns negativities and fears, and magically transforms human limitations. The shaman could also create a symbolic obstacle, like a hole in the ground in which he places objects that will be burnt. They represent the fear that holds people back, a fear felt by everybody. After lighting the fire, the shaman asks the participants to jump over or walk on this obstacle. The symbolism of this act is that the person goes beyond the fears that block him and whose existence he was previously unaware of.

In the direction West, it is possible to understand that at the time of death, the soul of the person journeys to an area of the Universe that is full of stars and remains there until it is time to return and reappear in a new incarnation. When we work in this direction we confront our deepest fears and it is wise to remember that if we do not work with them harmoniously this time, we confront them again in our next incarnation.

∞

When I was a child I suffered from several diseases that were related to my blood. Over time, I understood that my blood problems referred to karmic elements not being worked on. I had transferred these karmic energies to this present incarnation and the disease was an urgent message to render comprehensible to me these deep fears present in my life and to transform them and myself. It was this disease that I faced during my initiation in the Amazon. I needed to understand death in the literal sense and the fears that had created a real physical disease during my childhood. When I began my personal transformation, the chemical structure of my blood changed, allowing the karmic memory to release itself.

If during a disease the temperature rises unusually, this often means that the blood is undergoing a transformation: an urgent message indicating that something needs to be treated and changed. Blood and spirituality are symbolically associated (for instance, Jesus symbolically changed blood into wine at the Last Supper, an act that continues to this day in the Christian tradition of Communion). Blood is very symbolic and is related to our emotions; its fluidity is positive. During initiation, the karmic memory is transformed. Some South American people (e.g. Incas) often considered blood as our deepest connection with our ancestors. The blood sacrifices, of later generations of Incas, unfortunately perverted the idea of blood as being sacred.

As in the East, the West is associated (but in another manner) with the sun. In South America, during ancient ceremonies the whole city of Cusco was covered with gold in order to represent the power of the sun. People accomplished special rituals to allow the energy of the sun or the Great Spirit to come into the city. This Ceremony was supposed to help everybody in the community to go beyond his or her fears and to develop self-confidence.

It is towards the West that we must go because, finally, each one must face his own physical death. Symbolically the sunset expresses death. We all know that at the end of the day, the sun disappears into the vast night. However, each time the sun lies down, a change of consciousness, an inner reflection takes place. It is the time to put things in order, to relax the body into a state of sleep and to become one with the Spirit of the Night. It is the time when we can have strange dreams and see a different world other than the one we know during our waking hours. Death is basically the same thing as sleep. It is simply feared because it is unknown. When we work in the direction West we understand that the sun was never really touched or transformed by the darkness. To us it appears to lie down and rise again after the dark moments of the night, giving its light for a new day, a new beginning, like the phoenix rising from the ashes. But in reality the sun and its light is always there. We simply do not see it. To develop this comprehension in the work with death is a real achievement.

# Totem animals and Elements of Nature

In Huachuma shamanism, as in every shamanic tradition, all the elements of nature – animals, plants, rocks, mountains, etc. – play a central part in the well-being of the community. I believe that each living aspect of nature has a spirit and as such should be respected as a spiritual friend.

Animals are much more than just simple terrestrial creatures to which the status of 'domestic companion' is sometimes given. In a physical sense they are a vital "link" helping humanity to understand the secrets of Nature and return to their essential place of wholeness in and with the Universe.

Also, as the various stages of humanity's evolution include the evolution of the natural world, I believe all aspects of the natural world must be registered in our DNA. Thus it is that we can observe animals in nature, hear their messages for us and understand many things about them including the physical benefits of many medicinal herbs, healing foods and therapeutic exercises.

Some animals have a special significance, and they are totem animals. Their role is to help us in various situations that, in traditional societies, may mean life or death or that in the modern world may help us to get in touch with the more instinctual parts of ourselves that are lost.

Each area of the world has its own totem animals. Australian Aborigines might use the Spirit of the Kangaroo to guide them as they travel through their Dreamtime. Polynesians could have the spirit of the Whale as a guide on their long sea journeys. North American Indians may have for their totem an Eagle when they perform their Pipe Ceremonies. People of knowledge observe the power and behaviour of all these animals to understand better their harmonious place as one of Nature's children and thereby their impact on the world as they tread softly along their spiritual path.

For example, the Eagle in the Pipe Ceremony can help a person or the whole community to face a situation from a standpoint that is not that of the ego. It can rise very high in the sky (the sky representing the Higher Self) and fly away from the conflicts and personal dynamics, moving beyond the mundane and limited situations, which may be causing disharmony in the person or community. It has a completely different perspective on things (e.g. it can see the 'big picture' without it being obscured by the minor details).

∞

Totem animals, as our spiritual friends and guardians, can carry very important individual messages for us. They can highlight places of imbalance in our life. As most of us in the Western world are familiar with domestic animals let us use them for an example. For instance, a cat may lick a part of our body or a dog might remain unusually close to us for a long time. Whether we know it or not, what the animals are doing is truly shamanic: they are helping us to eradicate negative energies out of our body. We might be surprised to discover later on that at the exact place where the cat licked us, we have a problem of arthritis, or that the dog remained close to a part of our body which is now wounded. These animals saw imbalance before its concrete manifestation. As spiritual friends, they took the negative energies out of our body so that we could quickly get back into a state of balance. If we manage to understand what they, our animal totems, say to us, we can help ourselves before the imbalances appear.

Rather than simply being aware of the artificial environment that most of us in the modern world live in, it is perhaps more important to become aware of our totem animals and all of the elements of nature that come to us, either physically or in dreams, in order to stay in touch with and live in harmony with Mother Earth.

∞

In the Amazon, the lifestyle of the *Ayahuascero* communities that I lived with was intricately connected to the forest and all of its animals. As the *Ayahuasceros* consider the jaguar a totem animal, this means that the spirit of the Jaguar helps the community on a physical and spiritual level.

During the shamanic ritual of the *mesa*, (see the chapter "The Four Direction and the *Mesa*"), the shaman sings an *icaro*, his "song of power," and calls to the Spirit of the Jaguar asking it to be present in the ceremony. He speaks to the Jaguar as one speaks to a friend. Through this communication, he recognises the nature of the animal and becomes one with him. Actually, in many of the Amazonian languages, the words for 'shaman' and 'jaguar' are interchangeable.

With the force and the strength of the jaguar, whose spirit is not separate from his own, the shaman can move freely on the earth and in the water. The piercing eyes of this animal enable him to see in the dark, to climb trees, to observe the energy of the earth, the water and the sky and to be more easily in relationship with the natural world. Sometimes, the members of the community take part in this ritual and see that the shaman is going on a long journey into the forest. They see him like a jaguar. When the ceremony intensifies, they begin to ask him questions that can help the community to view the world in a completely different way by acquiring the perception, the force and the mental capacities of the animal. With their totem animal, the Jaguar, as a guide and a friend, the community members can thus learn, amongst other things, better ways of gathering food, of catching fish and of finding special places where they can collect important things (such as gold, medicinal plants, seeds, remedies etc).

As we don't live in the South American rainforest or jungle we would not expect to have such a relationship with a jaguar as the *Ayahuasceros*. However, we often see or sense in our dreams the spirits and/or energies of animals, of plants, of mountains, of rivers or of other things.

For example, a child may dream of a tiger. This means that he is dreaming about a part of his Self (possibly that part of himself afraid of growing up alone, separate from his parents and the comfort that he knows) which needs to be honored. Often, the child in his dream becomes afraid of this part of himself and runs away from the tiger in his dream rather than embracing the tiger, embracing the joy of growing up. When he wakes up, he is hot and sweaty and he feverishly tells his dream to his parents, from whom he seeks comfort. His parents, generally educated to believe that the tiger does not exist and the child, fully trustful of the opinion of his parents, doesn't realize that the tiger represents his own fears with which he is trying to come to terms and believes them when they say he has just had a "bad dream"... even if he still checks to see that there is no tiger hidden below his bed!

The mind of the child, which has not embraced the tiger, has now become programmed to be separate from this part of his deepest Self and this programming becomes a dimension of his personality. The tiger under the bed gets lost under the affect of civilization and, by adulthood, the feeling of separation and isolation has been reinforced. What this child is trying to escape is precisely what the shaman is being friendly with. The shaman does not experience separation but Totality.

To take this further, the child, who dreamed of being chased by a tiger, and who has now become an adult can continue to confront images or objects representing tigers or any other member of the cat family; each confrontation being an opportunity to transcend his childhood fears. He can become an archaeologist and be fascinated with the cats guarding the pyramids (places of initiation and transformation) in ancient Egypt, or be a veterinarian, wildlife photographer or zookeeper, or simply develop a hobby for collecting cats (books, stamps, porcelain, etc).

If this situation arose in a shamanic culture, the shaman might recommend a ceremony in order for the adult to recognize and make conscious this driving force behind his actions. During the ceremony the person is invited to enter into a more complete relationship with the tiger. He will then have an opportunity to let go of many situations that, through the years, separated him from the dream of the tiger that he had in his childhood. He might understand that in his dream he had faced a choice between trust (love) and fear. Choosing fear again, now, would mean continuing to escape, which at this stage leads nowhere. On the other hand, if he recognizes the tiger as an invaluable friend, a totem animal, and chooses to trust and love, to embrace and become one with the tiger, then he can learn with courage and strength how to trust that Life is nourishing us all of the time and belongs to all of us. In each situation evoking fear, the tiger can inspire him with confidence.

The action of the shaman in the Amazonian forest, with such issues, is a process of transformation towards Unity and Totality. This, I believe, has been lost for a long time in the West. The shaman's process of transformation is guided by the beautiful harmony of Nature - by its animals, its plants, its mountains, and its rocks because Nature can help us to understand that our inner world cannot be constantly maintained in the darkness of separation. In fact, Nature provides us with many of the solutions we seek if we are able to observe them as such. Life comes above all from a deep relationship with Nature, Mother Earth and the Cosmos. Totem animals, and other elements of nature are there, as spiritual friends, to help us gather the divided parts of ourselves.

In similar ways, such spiritual work can help others reclaim their lost connection with the Universe. Even if we do not live in the Amazonian forest, we need even more totem animals and elements of nature to assist us in the "urban jungle" in which we do live. Our body, our inner Being, needs to be connected to and in balance with the instinctual rhythms of Life.

The power of Nature can thus be evoked through a direct relationship with all of its aspects. Looking at a bird in the sky helps our body, mind and spirit to fly. In dreams we are able to fly because our cells have remembered this space of freedom. . It is important to understand that, in this experience of flying, we are not creating merely a mental relationship with a bird, or for that matter any other aspect of nature, instead we are actually reconnecting to our innate sense of freedom and our role in the Universe.

In reality, all the aspects of nature work in balance with a harmonious cosmos; if it were not the case, everything would collapse. When a part of our self is disturbed by fear and imbalance, Nature can remind us of its laws in a positive or negative way. We can, for example, dream of a sun burning and a sky so deprived of clouds that our world becomes an empty desert - the desert being a symbol of our lack of relationship to the external world - or we can fully accept the sunlight into our body, our mind and our emotions, so that our Spirit can shine just like the Sun.

With its compulsion to control Nature, civilization has forgotten the simple truth that by being one with the animals, the plants and the mountains, we embrace an important part of ourselves.

# Dreams

· · · · · · · · · · · · · · · · · · · ☆ ☆ ☆ · · · · · · · · · · · · · · · · · · ·

We are blessed to have dreams each night, even if we do not remember them. Dreams are beautiful messages along the path towards knowledge. Let us put the books aside, let us invite the ego (in its desperate drive to intellectualise every experience) to calm down and let us understand the way shamans work with dreams.

In Western societies, the ego has separated us from the world of dreams, thus separating us from an important part of our own reality. It is not so everywhere. In South American communities that have preserved traditional ways of living, dreams are a large part of everyday life. When children begin to speak, they already work with their dreams and that becomes a way of life. People sit in a circle and honor, by relating, their adventures of the night. Whatever the message, it indicates what one should do during the day. If the dream says to leave one's work, then let us leave it! But if Westerners acted this way, people around them would think that they were insane to take so seriously "a simple dream." Yet, we must live with the wisdom of our dreams.

To foolishly limit our actions to within a set of closed parameters prevents the magical and creative world within from touching our lives. Maybe by leaving the work where you feel stifled and bored you have a chance to discover a latent talent or a hidden potential never before considered. If the dream says to fly, let us fly!

When we understand the natural laws of a sacred dream we can fly. Our potential is unlimited. The question "Can you fly like an eagle?" addressed by the anthropologists to the shaman is for him out of place because in non-ordinary reality of course he can fly! Everybody can remember when they were a little child they wanted to jump out of the window or off the balcony and fly. Yet, when we tried flying we hurt ourselves. But we continued to believe in our dreams because we had more faith in them than in ourselves. In the inside world, there is a feeling of unity and magic telling us that everything is possible. Still aware of and very centered on their force of life, children know this better than adults. They continue to believe in the magic of the world they live in and in the creative life force that drives them in their actions.

Let us take our dreams seriously. If we dream we are flying, let us create a ritual that honors flying, let us dress like a condor, let us go to the mountains and symbolically let us learn how to fly. But if we think that it is impossible, we will not jump because of the fear of falling. To understand our dreams, it is necessary to put aside our ego and our conditioning and to approach the reality of the dream. People who have the courage to jump and to fly really do it in a non-physical dimension.

∞

Dreams can remind us of our path towards wholeness in this world. All the elements of a dream are parts of ourselves. Each time we dream of an animal or any part of Nature, we are close in spirit to the essence of ourselves. Let us listen to the power of Nature and understand its messages in our dreams.

The four elements representing the four directions of the *mesa* or the wheel of medicine – earth (East), fire (West), water (North), air (South) – are important aspects in the world of dreams. They give the keys for us to work with. I do say *to work with* and not simply *to interpret*. If, for example, one has a dream about the fear of changing an aspect of one's life, which works with the air and the wind in the direction South, then one can learn how to let go of the emotions because air is the element of change. Remember, the direction South has the snake as its symbolic animal, which assists the force of life (*kundalini*) to rise.

A dream can also tell us to eat a certain food to help the body on a physical level. This is because it is very important to work with the body. Also, for example, if we are angry, our body conveys this energy. Know that this state of being is temporary however, as the body and its cells constantly change with our level of consciousness. Also remember that when an emotional and spiritual change occurs the physical body must and will follow.

Dreams, even "bad ones," always tell us something good. They indicate that we are working with something very close to us. For example: a woman recounted to me a very short dream she had. In the dream she was lying down on the ground when a scorpion stung her in the area of her navel. She told me that, strangely, this bite did not give her any emotion or physical pain. For the shaman, the scorpion represents the direction East, the one concerned with the relationship between the body and the earth, and in the dream it was a messenger of the earth. The poison of the scorpion is a powerful medicine and this woman needed a strong medicine to purify her body, especially her blocked energy zones in the solar plexus, the stomach and the heart. Another example: if a dream implies that a tiger is pursuing you, the shaman will consider that the tiger has a very important message for you that needs to be understood urgently. Let us not flee away! Let us have courage! Let us befriend the tiger and speak with it. Let us enter the dream to grasp its unique language.

The more we work with dreams, the more we understand their complexity, the more they inform us at various levels of our awareness of their magic and the more they help us to become conscious of the knowledge and wisdom residing within all of us.

∞

We can use several tools to help us remember our dreams and then to work with them. For instance:

1. Have a pen and a book close to your bed so you can write your dreams down immediately on awakening. Remembering one's dreams is to respect them and to give them a physical dimension. People often postpone this act until later but then generally forget and do not find the time to do it. Finding the time to write some words down about the dream will initially remind us of its energy. It will then come back to us in images, feelings and sensations.

2. Use a tape recorder to verbally record the dream.

3. Draw or paint the dream.

4. Dance or create flowing movements that correspond to the energy of the dream.

5. Drink a glass of water to help remember your dreams. By that I mean, drink half of the glass before sleeping and the rest upon waking. This anchors the dream in the body, which sometimes cannot remember the details, especially when it is very tired or occupied or recovering from the past day.

6. Avoid looking at television before going to bed. After a working day we come back tired to the house, we turn on the television and this disturbs the rhythms of the brain. It disturbs the functioning of the pituitary gland (which helps to develop the sense of magic in us) and stops the natural flow of the dreams.

7. Take care of oneself before going to bed. Ritualise the transition from daily activities to sleep in a stress-free relaxed way.

8. Avoid engaging in a deep discussion about a problem and refrain from worrying thoughts before sleeping. The mind should be relaxed.

9. Relax oneself into the state of sleep by reading a spiritual book, inspirational words or sacred texts.

10. Make sure your bedroom is a quiet, clean and peaceful haven for sleep rather than an extension of your busy daily activities, unfinished work and/or life in general. It is nice to create an altar with simple and beautiful objects near your bed. Include positive objects, pictures and any other items you would like to invite into your dreams.

# Physical Types

· · · · · · · · · · · · · · · · · · · ☆ ☆ ☆ · · · · · · · · · · · · · · · · · · ·

Huachuma shamanism, in ancient times, classified humans into three basic physical types associated with their particular styles of food consumption. Each of us in theory then belongs to a specific type but, sometimes, a basic type can be combined with another. Of course, these three divisions are not strict. They simply provide an indication as to the way of refining our diets according to our body types.

## People with Round Heads

These people are very easily recognizable with their high cheekbones and their round heads. They generally have a strong and very developed stomach, because it is there that their life energy is localized. They are rather small and they tend to put on weight easily if their food does not correspond to their anatomy. This physical type is common throughout the world. It can be found in South-East Asia and the Arctic Circle, Siberia, and North and South America. The basic element of people with round heads is fire.

During their childhood, these people, being very physical, will probably run to explore things around them. They sometimes involve themselves in rather peaceful activities such as music and art. Full of energy, they are inclined to go forward very quickly, with the need to express themselves externally. They nevertheless are easily frustrated if their expression of themselves is in any way limited.

It is very important for their development that they feel nourished and safe. If their environment was relatively unstable when they were babies, if they did not receive what they needed when they needed it, they tend to bring an emotional negativity into their adult life. They are easily irritated when they are tense, which often happens to them. If they are not in harmony with themselves, their base chakra, generally strong, sends the energy towards the liver rather than towards higher chakras along the spine. The problems these people frequently develop with the liver are related to anger and sometimes to negative emotions (often disarming for others) that can animate them.

This physical type has its strengths and weaknesses. People with round heads tend to like things that taste sweet. However, if refined sugar as in chocolates and cakes provide the energy they need, this does not last very long. It only disturbs the blood system and the liver, which creates even more imbalance in their life. They must also consume proteins with moderation. Meat, eggs and some nuts cause them disharmony. Taken in moderation, these foods help the body to heal, but absorbed in excess they are very quickly transformed into energy and create disturbances and stress in the base chakra.

People having this physical type need to eat food that favors their well-being, providing a lot of energy to the body for a long period of time. They can balance their liver by eating many different seeds and cereals, bread, etc, very rich in minerals. With this food, they easily detoxify their liver and develop a greater balance in life. Red and orange foods, like tomatoes, paprikas, berries and marrows contain anti-oxidants (Vitamins C, etc.), which are very powerful for the liver. These are also very good for roundheads because, through their full and impassioned lives, they tend to weaken their blood systems which convey the energy (oxygen, nutrients) around their bodies.

Roundheads also have a particular attraction for foods which have a strong relation to the sun. These foods contain the life force of the sun. Sunflower seeds and fruits fit into this category. Indeed, these people have a tendency to be depressed or to be absorbed with the things they tend to see darkly negative. This is why the food of the sun is necessary as it allows the light to enter deeply into their cells. Cereals and other plants that naturally seek the light also bring precisely this intelligence into the physical body of these people and help them to transcend negativity.

Roundheads are inclined to work spiritually on themselves but their bodies can get depleted of minerals, in particular of calcium, when they face negative memories or blockages which prevent their deeper Self from being fully expressed. Calcium is thus especially important for them when they need to work with the past. It can be found in particular in sesame seeds, tofu, dairy products, etc.

## People with Long Heads and Oval Shaped Faces

People having this physical type are easily recognizable as the shape of their head is rather long. They can have round cheeks but they tend more to have rather oval shaped faces. They are found more frequently in the Middle East, in Eastern Europe, in certain parts of North America and Asia. Their basic element is water.

These people generally have a very strong solar plexus chakra and, in a similar way to people with round heads, they are full of energy. But rather than using this energy to express their inner Self, they turn towards the outside world. Very worried about the world that surrounds them, they generally have a problem with letting go of things. They forget to listen to their heart and to the deepest part of themselves. Because of their need to understand and to connect to the external world, they are easily inattentive and forget the powerful energy that moves inside them. They are therefore easily frustrated. Their frustration is normally not expressed through anger but through the weakness of their life energy. They tend to have a weak immune system and are likely to get sick. Their problem with letting go manifests itself in their emotional as well as in their physical life because they recover slowly from any disease they get. As they often do not take care of themselves, because of the hundred external things they must do, or understand, their kidneys are weak and work more than necessary. The more stress and distractions they have, the more it becomes chronic. If their kidneys remain weak for a long time, these people draw the energy from the thyroid gland. Many people with this physical type tend to suffer from thyroid problems, with an excess of weight and extreme changes of mood: all because the deepest aspect of their life energy is often unable to connect to the external environment in a whole and complete way.

Water, being the controlling element of the longheads, must be balanced in the body of these people but they tend to forget to drink and they eat very quickly in order to continue understanding the energy that is separate from them. They develop uric acid in their body that, with weak kidneys, is simply not able to always be totally eliminated. As a result, they generally direct their energy towards sexuality. Their sexual instincts are strong but often tend to be expressed in a way where the heart is not present: the bodies of these people simply release the uric acid and the excess of energy in their sexuality, which is often a source of problems for them.

Often gifted in professions of communication and therapies these people are nevertheless generally unable to communicate with the deepest aspects of themselves. When they suffer from disease, they have difficulty in helping themselves. The weakness of their thyroid means that they need to create more balance around the throat, in particular by learning how to *express* themselves in communication rather than simply *speaking*.

People having this physical type must definitely avoid tea, coffee, alcohol, sugar, white flour, very oily food (except olive oil), full fat cheeses and meat. All these tend to create an acid reaction in the body, which weakens the immune system and the kidneys and irritates the thyroid. This irritation is expressed in their emotions and also often in their spirituality.

The kidneys and the thyroid can be reinforced with specific foods including some types of cereals and green vegetables. Contrary to people with round heads, the best cereals here are those which create an alkaline reaction inside the body. In the Andes, the ancients (or "long heads") often used quinoa. In the Middle East and in some Mediterranean areas, the ancients used millet. Quinoa, millet and green vegetables help the uric acid to leave the system through the kidneys. The green vegetables not only cleanse the body but they also tend to change its acidity to a more balanced state, something that the kidneys generally cannot do alone.

Foods that are green and blue in color are the most appropriate for the longheads because they cleanse their bodies and strengthen their thyroid. This is enormously helpful for them in order to anchor themselves in their spiritual reality. These foods include peas, various kinds of beans, green, leafy vegetables, certain types of potatoes and root vegetables, pumpkins, blue-green algae, blueberries, etc.

Because of their connection with the element water, these people can be very introverted and see the world much more through subtle signs than through external logic. They have a connection with the moon and the world of dreams but, if they are not anchored in their spiritual reality, they do not seem to express their potential (in a creative way) in their existence.

## People with Square Heads and Large Flat Foreheads

People with very square heads and large foreheads (which are usually fairly flat contrasting with their faces) are easily recognizable and are frequently found in Central Europe and in various areas of Asia and the Pacific. Their basic element is air.

They tend to quickly use up their energy, which they have in abundance and spend much of their time feeling the world around them, rather than expressing themselves physically or intellectually. Those of this physical type seek harmony. When they were children their presence was probably very much appreciated by their parents. They tend to work in people-oriented professions, such as lawyers, human resources managers, etc. and are often very creative. Very diplomatic, they enjoy creating balanced lifestyles for themselves and the people around them. All disharmonies tend to weaken them, not only emotionally but also physically. They then suffer from colds, flu and allergies, which directly affect their respiratory systems, particularly their lungs and throats. They also tend to have problems with their hearts especially when emotional conflicts are internalized or when they lose their sense of purpose or meaning in life.

People having this physical type must consume dairy products in moderation because these foods increase mucous and aggravate their colds and/or flu symptoms. Their diet requires many concentrated foods, like seeds, nuts, oils, proteins and beans that favor the accumulation of energy in their body, thus avoiding drawing energy from the heart. Ideally, their foods must be yellow and gold in color.

∞

These three groups give a general idea of the characteristics associated with the different physical types and it is interesting to observe oneself, one's partner and one's friends to see how certain foods are, or are not appreciated. We can observe that different morphological types need things completely different from us. Let us not forget that the majority of people only have one physical type; however, others are sometimes a mixture of all three.

# Food

In Huachuma shamanism, food and the act of eating are fundamental for inner well-being and physical health. Food is not only a material substance that nourishes the body, but also a substance containing spiritual and emotional energy. Its energy is a very important source of life. It helps us to create a healthy foundation for our temple (our physical body), allowing inner work and transformation to take place quietly and harmoniously. This is why consuming food that is fresh and full of energy is central in this shamanic practice.

In Huachuma shamanism, the way we eat and what we eat mirror our spiritual development. It is never wise to buy canned or highly processed food, which is so common today on the television, in restaurants and fast food establishments, and on our shopping lists. How can this type of food contain the same life force as fresh vegetables and fruits? How can such a way of eating be spiritual? For the traditional populations of the Andes, these attitudes are horrifying and correspond to a slow death, an invitation for the physical body to easily get sick with age.

Huachuma shamanism considers that food is more than just a physical thing. Healthy food is not only for filling our stomachs because when eating it one communicates on a very deep level with Mother Nature. When we eat with more awareness, we understand that it is useless to refer to other people's ideas. When we are not dependent on the idea that food or the things of the external world can really fill us with happiness, we understand that in the natural laws, Happiness and what nourishes us, are an extension of Mother Earth, an extension of ourselves. The knowledge of Nature is acquired by understanding its laws and by being present to them.

I remember that in South America, in certain areas of the Andes, the people living a traditional life always ate food full of life energy. Their faces had a sparkle missing in Westerners of the same age. These people worked in the fields until they were 80 or 90 years old and did not have the symptoms of "old age." They lived on a simple vegetarian diet, breathing fresh air and showing joy and happiness in their tasks. Disease was rare and people often had many children. Many also lived for up to 120 years.

With all its technologies, its vitamin pills and its artificial medicines, the Western world does not experience this natural state of well-being still found in various parts of the world. Traditional societies are, however, being slowly touched by external influences. The Western diet is becoming prevalent throughout the world, thus we see the same diseases and lack of vitality, present in the West, now reaching the most isolated villages.

∞

Huachuma shamanism, alongside many other mystical traditions, does not recommend the consumption of meat and eggs. It considers vegetarian food as being the ideal way to have a healthy body. Being very acidic, meat tends to prevent harmonious digestion. For those who eat it, it is very important to eat it in association with many vegetables in order to neutralize its acidity. Generally, members of traditional cultures consume meat in very small quantities and always mixed with vegetables.

In the Amazon, meat and fish are important aspects of their diet but the quality of this meat and fish is very different from that found in supermarkets. Often the members of the community perform a ritual before hunting to communicate with the Spirit of the animal they will hunt, asking it whether it agrees to be sacrificed for the community. By doing this, they relate to a very deep level of the animal and ask whether its life force is compatible with their own. If the animal says "no" they will respect it (for example, it might be a mother animal that must take care of her young). If the men then continue to hunt that animal, kill it and eat it, then a negative reaction will occur in their bodies and they will understand they did something wrong to this animal and that that one should not eat the meat of an animal that has not agreed to be killed.

The animal can also say "yes" because it knows it is time for it to die and so the hunt can take place. When an animal says "yes" to its death, the person who kills it harmoniously works within the natural laws in the same way as the eagle preys upon the rabbit. In the West, we generally do not have such sensitivity; we eat meat or fish simply because we are accustomed to doing so.

When European pioneers arrived in North America, lacking the consideration of the Indians towards the buffaloes, they slaughtered thousands of them just for the pleasure of it. In a few years, almost all of the buffaloes were exterminated. Some were killed for their skins, others simply decomposed on the plains, which caused great distress to the Indians who realized that Europeans did not respect the animals nor did they work in agreement with the laws of Nature, in the same way as they did.

Many other animals throughout the world continue to know the same destiny. The animals, whose meat is bought in supermarkets, have generally been treated without any respect or affection during their lives or when they are killed. By not asking the animal if its life energy is compatible with ours, we break the natural laws. We only see this animal as being a material 'thing' and we are blind to its spiritual and emotional sides. Insensitive to the pain we inflict on Mother Earth and her creatures, we eat meat in the West almost by "cultural habit." At the same time we are hurting our own bodies by reducing our life force to a very basic material level and by incarnating the suffering of the consumed animal.

There is no comparison to eating meat bought in a supermarket to that of an animal, which has been ritually communicated with and hunted with the respect it deserves. The meat from the supermarket carries the disharmony, the suffering and the fear of the animal that was killed, which is then transmitted to our body. This can make us more aggressive and weaker, not only on the physical level but also on the spiritual and emotional levels. On the physical plane, "animals of consumption" have today had their life force tampered with by being fed or injected with multitudes of chemicals: antibiotics, colorings, tenderisers, preservatives, hormones, etc. This meat is very different from that which our great-grandparents would have eaten; their meat was chemical-free and came from animals that were raised in nature. Thus, one step to take would be to try and rear your own animals before consuming them, thus creating a relationship with the animal that is eaten. This would help us to realize that the meat we eat is not simply a material thing but contains a Spirit within it.

When we are in contact with the spirit or the life force of the foods we eat and when we work inside the natural laws, we understand that we have the choice to act against this force of life or in harmony with it. If we approach food from the point of view of the ego, we are likely to be insufficiently sensitive to the taste of what we consume. Rather than looking for the life force of the food, we trust the advice of the doctor or our culture, which only affirms the importance of having enough iron, protein, this or that. We listen to the external injunctions, rather than to the instinctual wisdom of our bodies.

If we are simply attentive to our Self, as we were when we were young children, we realize that we have an inner knowledge, which has evolved over millions of years in each cell of our body. The cells of the tongue, the mouth, the throat, the brain, the stomach, and the digestive system all have an intelligence that enables us to know which foods are good for our health. Babies can thus want to eat certain types of food because they understand instinctively that their body needs a specific life force so that they can be more in harmony with nature. Babies follow their inner feelings, as they have not been corrupted in the same way as adults, who are governed by ideas and beliefs coming from the external world,.

∞

Foods in season are the best for the body, the mind and the emotions. That which grows in the area where we live is naturally strong in vitamins, in minerals and nutritive factors that the body will need to pass harmoniously through the natural cycles. Even if we do not have any problems and if we believe ourselves to be in very good health, it is very important to provide the body with these nutritive factors to help it to reach a higher level of consciousness. In the process of personal and spiritual transformation, it is very important to eat foods in season. If we simply eat canned or imported foods from far away, much nutritional value will be missing and it will only support us on a material level.

The way in which we prepare food is also important. Food that is cooked in the microwave, or that is over-cooked, cooked with stress and without love, etc, is lacking in life force and taste.

The food suitable for the three physical types (See Chapter 'Physical Types') is often most available where the people of these types live. However, people living in South America may need to consume very different foods from those in Europe, even if their physical types are similar. This comes from the fact that foods heal weaknesses that are likely to appear amongst those who live in specific places. Contrary to the tropics where the cycles of nature are less harsh, in the northern and southern hemispheres food has specific qualities dependent on the climatic changes. Thus in the rainforest, the indigenous people eat a lot of starchy foods like yucca (American liliaceous) and sweet potatoes, whereas in the Andes, quinoa and corn constitute the basic foods. Whatever is needed, Nature provides in abundance.

During the changes of the seasons, nature offers specific foods to help bodies pass through the seasonal transitions and our tastes change accordingly. In the Northern hemisphere, during October and November, the blood, which symbolizes the energy of life, generally weakens for all of the three physical types. Nature then provides specific fruits and vegetables that naturally contain high levels of the relevant nutritive factors, which are important for strengthening the body at this time. The ancients living in the Mediterranean area thus considered the pomegranate very sacred. In abundance in these autumn months, its juice helps the body to remain in harmony with the cycles of nature. The nutritive elements contained in this fruit indeed reinforce blood for the long winter months during which one's general vitality can decrease. The body needs very different foods in fall, in winter, in spring, and in summer. All of the cycles through which our body passes are, as for the plants, related to the cycles of nature. When the weather is cold and rainy, the inhabitants of the Andes take a solid and hot food. When the weather is hot and dry, they then generally eat a cold and liquid food.

∞

To think that the food is "good" or "bad" diverts us from the relationship we naturally maintain with Mother Earth, the seasons, our own bodies, our intuition and our emotions. One should not stick to dogmatic and strict ideas about food. Let us follow our intuition on what our body needs! Rather than to simply judge that something is "good" or "bad," or to refer to books, we should listen to our body. When it is sick, we naturally seek some types of food that are wise to consume. The messages from the body must take precedence over those of the mind.

Our body is our temple. If, for instance, we continue to cover our food with salt and other such strong ingredients because it is what we are used to, then we are not learning the subtler tastes of the foods that our body-temple needs. It is very important to teach children to eat good food as soon as they are born, because their taste develops in the first three years. It helps them to develop intuitive tastes and knowledge of food. This is how it is in many indigenous societies and it is also one of the keys to vital strength and good health.

∞

Our emotional state when we eat is also important. Children can intuitively decide not to eat if joy is absent at mealtime. Accordingly, they may end up having a weak digestive system, which closes with stomach pains or with food disorders so painfully common nowadays. This will continue to have effects on them much later in life. If children do not want to eat during the family meal, and throw the food around them, etc., rather than becoming frustrated and angry, it is crucial that the parents set an example and express joy around the table. In this way the children are inclined to eat their food with the same joy.

Food must be good for one and should be consumed with joy. A joyous, relaxed body is the temple of the soul. When we eat a food with pleasure we absorb its life force. If we take pleasure in eating chocolates and cakes, then let us eat them! But while absorbing them, let us be present and conscious of what is really happening inside us. Food laden with taste enhancers, genetic modifications, salts and sugars can overwhelm our natural wisdom, but somewhere this wisdom remains alive. We must distinguish if the food we consume is a true expression of what nourishes us or if it is an addiction to compensate for what we really feel? We must cultivate discernment, guided by non-attachment to limiting behaviours, beliefs and sensations, but at the same time it is important not to be too extreme about food. I often see quite well-disposed vegetarians who have a whole set of rules about what is "good" and "bad". But, by seeing everything detached from their instinctual feelings, they have created, with their diet, a very fragile and unhealthy temple. In Huachuma shamanism, there are no dogmatic beliefs towards some types of diets, just simple ideas that provide guidelines of behavior for being in good health. It is the balance between good sense and spiritual attitudes that matters.

∞

Remember, Huachuma shamanism considers the body as essential in the process of transformation and particularly when one goes through emotional and spiritual changes. Traditional people speak about specific foods as very important and sacred referring to something fundamental related to the life force of this food. For example, if we eat dates, almonds, yoghurt and honey, four very sacred foods, we realize that they contain a beautiful energy of life that provides the body, mind and spirit with a life force totally different from that found in the chocolates, cakes and ice creams which are found in every supermarket. These sweet foods from the supermarket may seem very tempting, but what really occurs when these foods are ingested in the body?

If we believe that happiness lies in the gustatory pleasures that chocolate could provide, for instance, we will never find what we are looking for. When we are in touch with the life force of food (like that of fresh food), we realize that happiness cannot be sought apart from ourselves and we can easily break our addictions. We realize then that chocolate, sugar, coffee, alcohol, and cigarettes, for example, are not in this sense, good for us. These addictions are negative for the body; they do not bring any joy but simply provide a short moment of respite in the general discomfort and lack of plenitude we feel. When we start to taste food as it truly is, we find that things like sugar have a taste that is too crude and that all of our addictions are in reality an illusion.

This type of sensitivity is not always obvious when our capacities of discernment have been distorted by very strong tastes. The development of this sensitivity is part of the transformation of oneself. There is nothing "good" or "bad," What matters is the process, which makes us intuitively sensitive to the real essence of the foods we absorb.

∞

Indigenous people know that the foods, which carry the most life energy, are those such as seeds, grains and some tubers, which have an enormous power to proliferate. Second on the list are fruits and vegetables, which also have a marvellous force of life but do not have the power to grow like seeds. The energy of these foods being easily exhausted must be consumed fresh rather than canned or frozen.

We can check for ourselves if the life force of the food we buy is compatible with what we need for our body. If we take one minute to just experience the energy of, for example, an apple that we place between the palms of our hands, we could feel an energy movement appearing. If we consider that 0 means that we do not feel "any energy" and that 10 means the feeling of a "strong energy", we have then a scale from 0 to 10 to measure the energy of the life force between our hands. This can take time to learn at the beginning because the mind often interferes. Yet, with practice, we are surprised to find that a food we thought as healthy is actually, for some reason not compatible with our life force energy at all. This test can be extended to all of our material purchases. If we buy clothing made of nylon or polyester, those materials normally have a very low energy or an energy value of 0, compared to cotton or wool. This exercise is very simple yet very powerful. The problem is that we are always influenced by advertisements, cultural beliefs, what others (our parents, our friends, etc.) do and say and we do not always trust ourselves. The more we practice this energy test, the more we will be in harmony with our body and its life force. We can thus manage to buy many very different things from those we would normally buy.

Food affects everyone in the same way. We all constantly go through changes and food is a beautiful way of supporting and reinforcing this process of transformation. (Meat, chicken, and fish do not support this process in the same way as they do not transform the life force in our body.) As we become more sensitive, we realize that each food has a specific quality and affects our consciousness in a different way: wheat and corn have for instance a life force which raises us more towards the light; potatoes and other tubers rather draw us towards the earth. The food we eat interacts with our body and influences our life.

In indigenous communities, babies and children are never fed meat; rather they are given foods that contain more powerful life forces. Children can have goat's milk and even sometimes the milk of other animals to favor the development of their strengths. If they drink goat's milk they will have the same force, the same sense of adventure and same courage as the goat. If they drink Soya milk, the life force will be much weaker because this milk contains the energy of the Soya bean, which is quite energetic in itself, but not in tune with this stage of an under 5 year old child's development. This does not mean that Soya beans are not an important aspect of our diet, just that they are not suitable for babies. The action of Soya beans is in general very similar to that of meat. They are very rich in dense proteins and they convey the same heaviness and the same qualities as meat. They are not appropriate for babies because they draw their life energy and consciousness down to a very basic and material level. Ideally children must drink the milk of their mother for long enough to receive all of the qualities and subtle information necessary to be in good health. When they are old enough to drink another type of milk, they are then more in phase with animal's milk (especially goat's milk) than with that of plants.

If the mother feels that animal's milk is not good for her child, the traditional culture she lives in generally provides her with alternatives. The inhabitants of the Middle East were accustomed to producing very special milk made with almonds and certain herbs. Richer in minerals and calcium than most nuts or beans, almonds are regarded as a sacred food reinforcing many desirable qualities in the child. Convalescent children often take almond paste with a dash of honey and healing herbs. Of course, children in the Middle East would include tahini in their diet on a daily basis (also high in its calcium-rich milk-like qualities). Each food conveys a consciousness or intelligence inside and it is important that babies and children eat those foods that reinforce the necessary qualities for their optimum growth and harmonious levels of consciousness.

In the West we often believe that the quantity of food we eat is of more importance than its quality and thus we currently eat much more than the majority of the people of traditional societies. But these indigenous and traditional populations often eat much healthier and smaller portions of food, making their children stronger than Western children who, even if they consume food containing the right proportions of vitamins, proteins and minerals, still catch many of the so-called "childhood diseases." In my experience, the existence of these childhood diseases was minimal or non-existent among the communities I lived with.

∞

To close this chapter on food I would like to talk about a "Pyramid of Food" that is divided into four levels. It will give you some idea of a harmonious diet that will nurture your body while you are absorbing what is important in the food.

The base of the pyramid creates the foundation for our temple. To establish this foundation it is crucial to eat many chemical-free fresh fruits and vegetables in season and in particular those that grow locally. Chemical-free fresh fruits and vegetables are known to easily eliminate wastes and toxins, and to cleanse the mind and the physical body, which is a vital process in life. Without this food, the temple collapses. This is why one can never be in good health with only canned food and vitamin pills.

Take for example, tomatoes that have been locally cultivated and grown in a biological way, they have a completely different taste to those grown in greenhouses, full of chemicals, or worse genetically modified to obtain qualities having nothing to do with what "to nourish" means. It is difficult to taste the difference in the beginning but it becomes more obvious as you develop your sensitivity towards food.

The life force of food is obviously more present in fresh food than in that which is already several weeks old. This is why it is wise to include as much fresh food as possible in our diet. Pre-packaged food from the supermarket filled with salt, sugar, genetic modifications and other over-powering ingredients have lost their essence; their qualities and life force have been weakened.

Locally cultivated vegetables and fruits contain the nutritive elements and life force that should constitute the basis of our diet. When we eat vegetables it is important to remember not to mix vegetables and fruits in the same dish. However, baking fruit in the oven as a separate dish alongside, say, baked potatoes would be considered an exception.

The following fruits can be eaten fresh during meals: avocados, melons and papayas. (Note that red fruits eaten during the meal, or immediately after, generate problems of digestion, as they are very acidic.)

When preparing vegetables, they should not be over-boiled because this causes the loss of many of the vital elements necessary for healthy digestion. In many South American communities, and similarly in Polynesia, the traditional way to cook vegetables was very slowly. The foods were wrapped in leaves from specific plants or trees and buried in the earth above hot stones. Slowly and slightly cooked over several hours, the food (cooked with the four elements: the fire to burn the wood and heat the stones, the earth as the oven, the water from the vapour coming out from the heated vegetables, and the air circulating inside the oven) was very digestible. In the West, to achieve similar results, we could use unglazed clay dishes to bake our food in, to preserve the delicious and subtle qualities, while slowly cooking our meal.

∞

On the second level of the pyramid there are cereals and seeds. These foods tend to grow towards the light and contain several special strengthening minerals. Known to develop the body, they are very important in specific situations, such as when a child is growing fast or when an adult carries out much physical work. After a disease, during convalescence, these foods are invaluable for the body, not only to rebuild it but also to bring more light into the functioning of the cells. They normally have a strong protein level when they are mixed with vegetables. Cereals and legumes combined constitute an ideal source of protein.

∞

On the third level of the pyramid are the tubers like sweet potatoes and the roots like carrots, which all grow under the ground. These foods are particularly important during the winter and after long periods of disease, because they provide good substance for the body. They also are frequently used after Ceremonies to ground the physical and spiritual bodies.

The third level foods are NOT very good for children under five years old, as they redirect the energy of the life force towards the base chakra which is better developed at around 6 or 7 years old when the child comes more into contact with material energies. As they contain a denser quality of minerals than fresh vegetables, they are important at the times when the seasons change and in situations where the diet requires such minerals.

∞

The top (or fourth level) of the pyramid contains the full protein and sweet foods, like nuts, seeds, beans, legumes, dried fruits, dates, raisins, dairy products, milk, cheese, yoghurt, tofu, tempeh, honey, and mushrooms. If consumed, meat, fish and eggs are also included in this level of the pyramid. These foods must be consumed in moderation because they consist of concentrated proteins and energy. They are important for children as well as in cases of debilitating diseases.

The general action of beans and all legumes upon our bodies is very similar to meat. I don't include them in my food, as I believe they inhibit the subtler, beautifying qualities encouraged by fruits and vegetables. Some of the most important vegetables that encourage these subtle, beautifying qualities and which I include daily in my diet are sea vegetables such as Arame, Nori, Hijiki, Dulse and Powdered Kelp, and algae such as Chlorella and Spirulina. These are especially important for women who are pregnant or breast feeding.

∞

I consider that we must include as many "*sacred foods*" as possible in our diet such as honey, pollen, almonds, pine nuts, dates, grapes, pomegranates, coconuts, sesame seeds, quinoa, milk and carob. These sacred foods contain many trace minerals that the body needs:

- Milk (cow, goat, sheep, buffalo, etc.) is sacred and is for me one of the foods of the gods. However, it was never meant to be absorbed in its pure state but in the form of yoghurt, curdled milk or "*kefir*" or in the many ways imagined by the ancients. Taken curdled, it has a very spiritual quality and is excellent for children. The milk our ancestors drank and that members of traditional societies still often drink today is very different from the milk bought in supermarkets. Supermarket milk contains very little life force and is full of chemicals, antibiotics and hormones, which often cause allergies and reactions to those who consume it.
- Dates and carob provide a rich source of minerals, especially iron and magnesium and possess a healthy sweetness.
- Almonds and pine nuts are excellent for reinforcing the body, especially during times of convalescence and fatigue.
- Pomegranates, grapes and coconuts are good for anaemia and for cleansing and strengthening the blood.
- Honey is an excellent antibiotic and, in small quantities, a powerfully cleansing and healing food.
- Sesame is rich in calcium and iron and particularly alkalising to the body.
- Pollen is a super food with almost every known nutritive factor present in a dense and easily digestible form.
- Quinoa, especially sprouted quinoa, is an excellent strengthening food, similar to millet.

Most of the sacred foods are located in the top level of the pyramid because if they are consumed in excess they tend to be too strong for the body*.

∞

Please remember that in Huachuma shamanism, before eating, as a sign of respect towards the earth and to be present to the food and its origin, a little food should be put aside for Mother Earth. Also, the process of eating should be quiet and joyful. With each mouthful, one should be fully conscious of the food. To eat is not simply a physical process, rather a whole process of enhancement and development.

---

* For more comprehensive information about sacred foods and kefir you may like to read the booklets "Sacred Foods" and "Kefir", also by Tony Samara (see website: www.samarafoundation.com)

# Energy Postures

Huachuma shamanism uses energy postures to help the body to adjust physically, emotionally and spiritually to the cycles of nature. These postures are very similar to those of Tai Chi and Yoga and I believe them to be older. If we look attentively at some of the symbols and drawings on the ruins of very ancient South American temples, as well as in Egypt, we see humans and animals in unusual postures. When regularly practicing these postures we understand their meanings. They are not only useful to help our physical body to become stronger but also to adjust emotionally and spiritually and to develop our inner power in relation to that of Mother Earth. These exercises are particularly advantageous at certain times of the day because energies are different in the morning, in the afternoon and in the night.

**Here are ten basic exercises that shamans and ancient people have been practicing for thousands of years.**

## 1. Clearing Energy

*This very simple exercise helps the body to release energy. It can be practiced at any time when one feels overwhelmed or stressed by external circumstances.*

Stand in a relaxed fashion. Take a few deep in and out breaths through the nose. Continue to breathe deeply, in rhythm with the following movement. Visualize the stress and overwhelming energy clearing while shaking the whole body, especially the hands, for a few seconds. Repeat the exercise three or four times, making sure that all of the tension around the face and the jaw completely disappears with the shaking movement. (It may help to sigh as you shake.)

## 2. Walking Meditation

*One of my favourite exercises suitable for old and young alike is walking. For preservation of health and the prolongation of life, walking in the open air with abundant sunshine is a gift that is one of the surest safeguards against disease. As we absorb the elixirs of life in fresh air the blood becomes cleaner, the mind becomes more pure and forgotten vitality returns to the body, mind and spirit.*

Walk comfortably, breathing in and out with total awareness. Synchronise your breathing with the rhythm and pace of your movements. Be aware of all the sounds and elements of nature that surround you. Allow your mind to rest and immerse yourself in the aliveness of Life. Do this for 20 minutes or more at least once a day.

## 3. Grounding Exercise

*This exercise helps to ground the energy that is in the area around the head directing it down towards the base chakra. It is not good for those who have spine or neck problems.*

Stand in a relaxed fashion. Gently raise the body up from the ground onto the balls of the feet. Suddenly, come back down to the initial relaxed standing position with the heels striking the ground in a firm yet gentle manner. The body should be completely relaxed throughout the exercise. Inhale through the nose as you rise onto the balls of your feet and exhale as you come down onto your heels, chanting the sound *'hu.'* Repeat the exercise three or four times whenever it is needed.

## 4. The Tree Exercise

*This exercise is particularly important to do when feeling overwhelmed by negative thoughts (your own or those of other people around you) as it helps to gently drain away those negative energies in order to come back to a more balanced and harmonious state of being.*

Find, or visualize, a beautiful tree and squat in front of it. With both hands hold onto the trunk of the tree, keeping the body balanced as you do so. It is also possible to do this standing upright if it is difficult to squat. Visualize the positive strength of the tree helping you to let go of all that is overwhelming you in life. Feel the energetic imbalances slowly move out from your body. (These imbalances will penetrate into the trunk of the tree from your hands and will sink down through its roots back into the earth, where Mother Earth will transform it into a balanced energy.) Then take a deep breath in through the nose and, with every in-breath feel the life force of the tree strengthening and supporting your whole body (in particular the spine) and feel a tingling sensation moving throughout your body. Continue to breathe and feel completely at one with the spirit of the tree. As a sign of respect and thankfulness to the tree, leave a simple gift, which can be corn, sage, a flower, any herb or crystal, showing your appreciation for the healing that the tree has given you.

## 5. Strengthening the Heart

*This exercise is particularly good between 4 am and 5 am.*

Sit down with legs crossed comfortably on a cushion with the back upright. Release the shoulders. Close the eyes. Breathe slowly and deeply. When starting to feel quiet, direct the consciousness towards the area of the heart and place the hands in a relaxed way on the knees, palms upwards. While taking a deep in-breath through the nose using the lower part of the lungs (towards the abdomen), join together the thumb and the middle fingertips together on both hands and squeeze gently. With each out-breath through the mouth, relax the whole body and let go using a *hum* sound. It is important to prolong the breath and the sound. Repeat this exercise for 15-20 minutes.

## 6. The Liver Exercise

*This very powerful exercise is particularly good for detoxifying the body. The ideal moments to practice it are at sunrise and/or sunset.*

Stand facing the sun and relax the body. Slightly bend the knees with the feet about shoulder width apart and the eyes comfortably looking towards the sky. While breathing in through the nose, visualize (with eyes open or closed) the energy of the sun coming into the body, towards the solar plexus area (just above the navel). Gently bring the hands together (one on top of the other) on the solar plexus. Exhale with the mouth making a prolonged *aahh* sound and pay attention to the liver area. Visualise the liver opening itself to release the toxins. Feel the energy of the sun bathing the liver with heat, warmth and light. Repeat for a few minutes.

## 7. The Bear Position

*This position strengthens the abdomen, the intestines, and the ankles and adds tone to the body. It is particularly good for those who have problems of constipation and fragile stomachs. For women, it will also facilitate their giving birth but don't overdo it! The best time to practice the exercise is between 8 am and 9 am. (Note: this exercise is not recommended for those with hemorrhoids.)*

a) (Simplified form for a child.) Squat down on a flat surface with the heels and toes on the ground; the weight of the body should be close to the ground. Keeping the back straight, with the hands on the chest above the knees, look straight ahead. Breathe in a relaxed way, making sure that the face and shoulders are completely at ease and relaxed.

b) The most advanced form of this position is not suitable for those who suffer from lower back pain. From the above simple position, lift up onto the balls of the feet, the body balancing on its toes. Only the zone around the ankles is in tension, the rest of the body should be totally relaxed. The breathing must be deep and make sure that the lower part of the body is touching the heels. Once one starts to feel relaxed in this position, move the hands from the chest upward towards the shoulders, gently leaning the elbows onto the knees and continuing to face straight ahead. Stay in the position for a little while, breathing easily all the time.

## 8. Third Eye Meditation

*This exercise makes energy go up along the spine towards the third eye. It is particularly good at around 1:30 pm, but not recommended for those who suffer from lower back problems.*

Sit down comfortably crossed-legged on the ground. Straighten the back, pushing the chest out and keeping the head perfectly aligned with the spine. Bring your hands to the back of the neck, interlocking the fingers together. Take a deep in-breath through the nose and, while exhaling through the nose (or the mouth), direct the forehead down to the ground, (bending from the hips rather than from the waist) touching it if possible. Maintain this position as long as possible while holding the breath out. When the need to breathe in or the feeling of getting uncomfortable begins, gently bring back the body to an upright position, slowly breathing in and visualizing the third eye opening; feel the energy circulating throughout the whole body. Repeat the exercise 5 to 10 times.

## 9. The Gland Exercises

*These are in four stages that seem very important to me not only for physical health but also to protect the whole emotional and energetic body from the bombardment of daily stresses. These exercises invigorate the glands of the body and help you to feel and stay young. They are very good to do between 5 pm and 7 pm.*

1. Find a comfortable sitting position, preferably on the ground. Keep the back straight and the head upright. Make sure the shoulders are relaxed and any tension in the face is released (especially check the jaws). Close the eyes, take a deep breath in through the nose and, while exhaling (with the nose or the mouth), let go again. While taking another deep breath, fill the whole body with air and let go again. With the third breath, fill the whole body with air while counting up to 7. Then retain the breath while counting up to 2. Gently exhale while counting up to 7, making sure that all the air remaining in the body is completely -expelled. Retain the empty lungs for the count of 2. Repeat the in-breath while counting up to 7 and so continue this exercise (7-2-7-2) several times. After finishing this exercise (approximately 5 minutes) move onto the next one.

   *This exercise helps to correct disturbances in the body's natural chemistry and once these disturbances are corrected the body's own healing forces become more alive and vital.*

2. Keeping the eyes closed, simply feel (or visualize) the energy in the body as an inner movement rising from the base of the spine; sway the whole body from side to side or, if preferred, in a gentle, circular motion. Breathe deeply in and out. The spine and the head are straight and only

the base of the spine moves giving a soft circular motion to the trunk. The movement should come naturally from the base of the spine. While doing the exercise, place the tip of the tongue on the higher part of the palate, behind the teeth. You may want to accompany this with a *humming* sound. The complete exercise can be done for 5 to 10 minutes or longer if one feels at ease.

*At some point when doing this movement, or perhaps at the end of it, one can feel a little light-headed or have an unusual sensation. This is a good sign as it means that the sixth chakra (the third eye) and the seventh chakra (often called the crown chakra) are opening because this exercise activates the pituitary and pineal glands. These glands are considered essential for spiritual growth. The exercise also activates an increase by the brain of the production of a special fluid that starts diffusing down into the physical body. This fluid is very important for transforming the cells of the body and allowing them to accompany each person's transformation and spiritual growth. This process of transformation works naturally in babies and children, but is lost with age when the ego takes over and we begin to see the world as limited. In adults the pituitary and pineal glands generally function to a much lesser degree than in the newborn baby. Indeed, the more we function with our ego, the more this fluid decreases and the pituitary and pineal glands shrink. However, these glands will remain active only in adults who do a lot of meditation, contemplation, chanting and various Yoga or Tai Chi movements. These glands are also very active in spiritual people who tend to have this fluid emanating from their whole body. As the fluid begins to move downwards into the throat (this may not be obvious until one is more sensitive to subtle sensations), one can move on to the following exercise.*

**3.** Again, make sure that the body is relaxed and the shoulders are drooping. Breathe in through the nose, and gently move the head backwards, feeling the whole neck stretching until it naturally rests backwards with the eyes facing up. Then gently and slowly, breathing out, bring the head back to an upright position, then slowly and gently bringing the head forward until the chin rests on the chest. The shoulders must be relaxed. While breathing in, bring the head back to an upright position and, breathing out, lean it to the right with the eyes facing straight ahead. Keep the position until feeling the opposite side of the neck completely stretched and the head almost rests on the right shoulder. Breathe in and gently bring the head back to an upright position. Exhale and lean the head towards the left shoulder until the opposite side of the neck is completely stretched and flexible. Breathe in and bring the head back to an upright position again. Repeat the exercise several times, and then move on to the last one.

*While repeating this exercise, one feels the neck become stretched and more flexible. The movements of the head reinforce the thyroid (it being the center of the energy of communication), help to balance the physical body by strengthening the immune system, and also allow weight loss t if overweight, or weight gain if underweight. This exercise also balances the emotions and helps to manifest one's spiritual comprehension and wisdom in a communicative form. Thus, instead of talking about the weather one may find oneself talking about more profound and important things. The exercise also helps to open the throat chakra and we may feel and experience deep emotions that we were unaware of before. This is a good sign and part of the process of transformation. While communicating more deeply with oneself and the world, one strengthens a more profound part of oneself.*

4. Take a few deep breaths and relax the body. Bring the right or left hand or both to the area at the top of the rib cage (sternum) and, gently and rapidly tap with the fingertips on this area. Repeat for a few minutes breathing deeply into this area and relaxing or making the sound *aahh* on the out breath. When the exercise is completed, close the eyes for a while but become aware of the environment, of the sounds around you. Then, slowly, still breathing deeply, prepare to come back to the everyday world.

*Doing this for a few minutes will help the fluid from the throat to move down into the heart and to disperse throughout the physical body. This helps the spiritual and emotional aspects of our Self to be grounded in the physical body. It also helps to assist the immune system and strengthens the heart and lungs. Finally it helps us to prepare in a more balanced way for deep changes to happen within us.*

## 10. The Exercise of the Eagle

*This posture is used to locate lost objects and to help remember forgotten memories. It was used frequently in South America during initiations, when the shamans were tested to find objects or buried treasures. It is very good to practice it between 8 pm and 10 pm, when the mind is especially receptive.*

Find a quiet place where it is possible to be left undisturbed for 5 to 10 minutes. Stand with your hands relaxed at both sides of your body and your head facing forward. Relax your shoulders. Gently close your eyes and visualize your body starting to change, becoming one with an eagle. While breathing in through your nose, bring your arms out from your sides up to the height of your shoulders, with your fingers pointing towards the ground. On the next in breath, feel your whole body begin to gently sway and, with your eyes still closed, imagine your body starting to fly. Imagine you are observing everything as you fly around. When your arms begin to get tired, they can relax gently towards the sides of your body. Continue slightly swaying while concentrating on your third eye. Simply be present, without trying to do anything specific. Just feel the swaying of your body leading you deeper and deeper to being present to something that is needed.

What you think you need to find may be completely different from what the eagle helps you to discover. Just be present to the process and allow the information to come through to you without logically or analytically making sense of it. Stay in this position for as long as you need.

# Epilogue

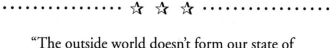

"The outside world doesn't form our state of consciousness rather it challenges us to make a choice.

A choice where we hear the voice of truth as it gently invites us away from the madness that we have created for ourselves. A choice that invites us to transcend the world of the unconscious by remaining fully absorbed in the present moment.

As we make each full and complete breath with awareness we take our greatest leap towards enlightenment dis-identifying from that which limits us from being totally present.

In the present moment we live in a limitless dimension of magical possibilities, all leading to the adventure of growth as we excite our hearts and experience true freedom."

*Extract from*
*"From the Heart – The Teachings of Tony Samara, Volume I"*

# Glossary

**AWARENESS** - a state of presence, a feeling of oneness with one's surroundings, being able to understand beyond the social, cultural or ego limitation of the senses and the mind.

**AYAHUASCA** - a sacred mind-altering drink believed to help individuals to perceive energies and realities not normally perceived in ordinary reality.

**BALANCE** - harmonious, peaceful loving existence in connection and interaction with one's surroundings and one's inner world.

**CHAKRA** - energetic center located in both physical and energetic body connected to nervous system in spine.

**ILLUSION** - living a program, an idea, a thought, a feeling rather than acknowledging what is directly present in our lives.

**INITIATION** - a ritual that allows the initiate into the world of mystery beyond a normal experience, a direct transference of knowledge.

**KARMA** - all actions, thoughts, feelings create a reaction equal to original in its strength but not necessarily in quality.

**MEDICINE WHEEL** - an orientation map often connected to cosmic and astrological forces as well as to earthly forces.

**MESA** - a South American Medicine wheel with various cultural symbols, often used in ritualistic healings.

**PROCESS** - when unable to see one's reality, whether emotional, mental or energetic and then transferring it onto a situation, a person, culture or group of people in a negative way.

**SAN PEDRO** - a sacred, mildly mind-altering drink used for healing and to perceive the depth and complexity of the world on various levels.

**SHAMAN** - a healer initiated into another understanding of sickness and suffering.

**SHAMANISM** - a culture that has shamans and understands sickness and suffering from a shaman's perception.

**ZEN BUDDHISM** - a Japanese tradition of meditation that emphasizes direct experience, perception of how to be free from karma and find peace.

"SHAMAN'S WISDOM" presents in a simple and practical way, universal shamanic knowledge that Tony Samara learned and experienced throughout his path to initiation. From the consumption of food to working with dreams, the four elements and the cardinal points, the presentation of some respiratory and physical exercises which support spiritual development, as well as many other topics, this book reminds us of positive ancestral wisdoms, more useful than ever in today's world. Help yourself to change your life for the better.

*"The shaman can start to work as healer only when he goes through what is called an experience of death/rebirth, the death of the suffering and rebirth to a new way of seeing things, where the point of reference is not any more the ego but the Cosmos; everything being connected to everything. During the initiation, I was given Ayahuasca and a terrible storm seized the forest and me. I had the greatest fear of my life. All my body disintegrated. I had the feeling to die. I called upon the gods from various religions, in vain. A large snake appeared and started to swallow me. I understood that it represented the pulsation of the energy of the Universe. I was not afraid to die anymore. I had lost the sense of the surrounding world. My body had become a part of the Universe. I developed a feeling of unity. This initiation changed all my perceptions of reality. Released of my past programming, my spirit was able to live the magic and joy of existence."*

*Tony Samara*

# FINDHORN PRESS

*Books, Card Sets,
CDs & DVDs
that inspire and uplift*

For a complete catalogue,
please contact:

Findhorn Press Ltd
305a The Park, Findhorn
Forres IV36 3TE
Scotland, UK

*t* +44-(0)1309-690582
*f* +44-(0)1309-690036
*e* info@findhornpress.com

or consult our catalogue online
(with secure order facility) on
www.findhornpress.com

For information on the Findhorn Foundation:
www.findhorn.org